Apologetic Preaching

Proclaiming Christ to a Postmodern World

Craig A. Loscalzo

InterVarsity Press
Downers Grove, Illinois

InterVarsity Press
P.O. Box 1400, Downers Grove, IL 60515
World Wide Web: www.ivpress.com
E-mail: mail@ivpress.com

InterVarsity Press® *is the book-publishing division of InterVarsity Christian Fellowship/USA*®, *a student movement active on campus at hundreds of universities, colleges and schools of nursing in the United States of America, and a member movement of the International Fellowship of Evangelical Students. For information about local and regional activities, write Public Relations Dept., InterVarsity Christian Fellowship/USA, 6400 Schroeder Rd., P.O. Box 7895, Madison, WI 53707-7895.*

Scripture quotations, unless otherwise noted, are from the New Revised Standard Version of the Bible, *copyright* © *1989 by the Division of Christian Education of the National Council of the Churches of Christ in the USA. Used by permission. All rights reserved.*

The sermon found on pages 94-99 is taken from "What Is Truth? Or Shirley MacLaine, Meet the Master" by John Killinger from Best Sermons 1, *edited by James W. Cox. Copyright* © *1988 by James W. Cox. Reprinted by permission of HarperCollins Publishers, Inc.*

Cover photograph: Michael Denora/Tony Stone Images

ISBN 0-8308-1575-9

Printed in the United States of America

Library of Congress Cataloging-in-Publication Data

Loscalzo, Craig A.
  Apologetic preaching: proclaiming Christ to a postmodern world/Craig A. Loscalzo.
    p. cm.
  Includes bibliographical references.
  ISBN 0-8308-1575-9 (paper: alk. paper)
  1. Preaching. 2. Apologetics. 3. Postmodernism—Religious aspects—Christianity. I.
Title.
  BV4211.2.L6737 2000
  251—dc21   *99-086868*

19	18	17	16	15	14	13	12	11	10	9	8	7	6	5	4	3	2	1
15	14	13	12	11	10	09	08	07	06	05	04	03	02	01	00			

To the Immanuel Baptist Church Ministry Team
partners in ministry

CONTENTS

Acknowledgments

In preaching a sermon from 1 Peter, I became captivated by Peter's admonition in chapter 3: "But in your hearts sanctify Christ as Lord. Always be ready to make your defense to anyone who demands from you an accounting for the hope that is in you; yet do it with gentleness and reverence" (vv. 15–16). While teaching preaching, and now in finding myself in a pastorate, I became convinced of the need for preachers to put away milquetoast sermons and take Peter's advice to the pulpit. This passage formed the foundation for my preaching in the closing years of the second millennium. It has also forged my understanding of apologetics. This book grew out of a desire to provide preachers help in making a defense to anyone who asks for an accounting of the hope that we have in Jesus Christ.

Special thanks go to Glen Cummins, Steven Gray, David Howard, Steven James, Paul Schultz, Mark Smith, James Stillwell, Dianna Stone, Barbara Walker and Joan Watkins—the ministry team to whom this work is dedicated. Through their ministries, their friendship and their teamwork, they have helped me shape my understanding of preaching more than they will ever know.

Thanks also go to the congregation of Immanuel Baptist Church in Lexington, Kentucky, the church I have served as pastor since Palm Sunday 1996. They provide constant love and encouragement that make preaching the gospel a continual joy and labor of love.

I also want to express my gratitude to the editorial staff at InterVarsity Press, for their encouragement in this project and for guiding it through the publication maze to completion. Their patience with me when I made the transition from the classroom back into the parish went far beyond grace. For that they have my deepest thanks.

Saving the best for last, I want to express my love and appreciation to my wife, Aunchalee, for her encouragement to persevere when this manuscript hit ruts and seemed as if it would never come to completion. She is truly my partner in ministry.

I thank my God for the call he has placed on my life to preach the gospel of Jesus Christ.

1

Apologizing for God: Apologetic Preaching to a Postmodern World

Acartoon displayed on my office door portrays a pastor, sitting behind a large wooden desk, being consoled by an obviously caring parishioner. The pastor's face betrays disappointment and discouragement. A "Worship Attendance Chart," prominent on the wall behind the desk, has apparently provoked the pastor's heavy anxiety and dismay. The chart shows a steep decline in worship attendance over the past two years; soon the descending line will extend beyond the chart's boundaries. The parishioner, in model pastoral-care tone, suggests, "I'm no expert . . . but perhaps you shouldn't close each sermon with 'But then again, what do I know?'"

Preaching Between Times

The pastor and the parishioner reflect the angst of today's preaching situation. We live and preach between times. The dogmatism of the modern era's pulpit has given way to ambivalence in pulpits of the postmodern era. In the presence of political correctness on one side and the fear of sounding like a rabid fundamentalist on the other, preachers skulk from their studies to the

pulpit, wide-eyed and confused, like children facing their first day in school.
The children's fear appears warranted, for they will truly enter an unknown
world. But preachers cannot hide behind such childlike apprehension, because we have been to the pulpit before, and the fear we face is often of our
own making.

We fear successful megachurches that have marketed their programs
well, attracting parishioners from among the baby boomers and baby
busters in our communities and even from our churches. We fear church
apathy and lethargy. The empty pews in our line of sight Sunday after
Sunday do nothing to quell such fear. Yet we also fear what might happen
if we pushed too hard or demanded too much. We fear being labeled narrow-minded by colleagues, by the media, by academics under whom we
studied while pursuing theological education and by our educated church
members who remind us, in many subtle ways, who pays our salary.
Words like *sin, judgment, immoral, evil, righteousness, faith* and *commitment* have been purged from our progressive ecclesiastical vocabulary.
We fear their use might rupture our hearers' boundaries and offend their
sensibilities. We fear being stereotyped with both the religious right and
the religious left. We have become so hypercautious that our sermons at
best offend no one and at worst merely bore. We fear being irrelevant, so
our sermons become mundane chatter about raising self-actualized children or coping with the latest midlife crisis or providing five easy steps
for managing anxiety.

The role of one who introduces people to mystery runs counter to everything we hear or read about so-called successful ministers and churches.
Though we cringe at the notion of being successful, we fear the alternative
even more. In our ubiquitous fear, apologizing for God rather than coura-
geously proclaiming the gospel, in all of its scandalous stead, becomes our
sermon fare.

Frightened as we are, we live and preach between times. The modern
world passes; in bursts the postmodern world. "We're not in Kansas anymore," announces Dorothy. I think she's right.

The Landscape of the Postmodern World

If my thesis about preaching between times is correct, what does this *mean-time* look like? What makes up this dawning postmodern world, and how will we know it when we see it? Will there even be preaching in postmodernism?

Well, the speculation hinges, of course, on how one defines *postmodern*. Definitions of the term abound. A current flood of books, journals and doctoral dissertations use *postmodern* as though it had a fixed meaning to which every thinking person ascribed. Such pondering is a paradox, because one characteristic of postmodernism is its intentional willingness not to objectify anything.

Is postmodernism a movement, a philosophy, a reaction to modernism or merely a modern shibboleth academicians use to impress other academicians? The answer: all of the above. A dictionary definition might describe postmodernism as a reactive movement against the theories and practices of modern art, literature, philosophy, economics, politics and theology. Calling postmodernism merely "a reactive movement," however, begs some larger issues at stake. In a basic and sweeping sense, postmodern is what follows modern. Thomas Oden offers a helpful framework by dating modernity from 1789 to 1989, what he calls "from the Bastille to the Berlin Wall."[1] So one definition of postmodernity is that period which follows modernity.

But is *postmodernism* merely a temporal term—a turn of the calendar page, a kind word to describe the death of an aging era—or is there more going on in the caldron of time and space than meets our modernity-conditioned eyes? Homiletician David Buttrick suggests we live "in the midst of a cultural breakdown not dissimilar to the collapse of the Greco-Roman world or the fragmentation of the Medieval synthesis."[2] Is this description of our cultural milieu mere hyperbolic musing? Or are we truly experiencing the disintegration of the existing world order—a system to which we might owe more allegiance than we care to admit? Diogenes Allen states: "A massive intellectual revolution is taking place that is per-haps as great as that which marked off the modern world from the Middle Ages. The foundations of the modern world are collapsing, and we are entering a post-

modern world. The principles forged during the Enlightenment (c. 1600–
1780), which formed the foundations of the modern mentality, are crum-
bling."[3]

One would have to live as a hermit not to personally experience the anxiety enveloping modern, or should I say postmodern, living. Increased violence mars our cities. Teenagers, even churchgoing teenagers, appear
oblivious to the moral moorings that once seemed to hold our culture from
going adrift. Heightened racial and ethnic tensions splinter what used to be
sane communities. "We live in systems that no longer work," bemoans Buttrick, "a politics of gridlock, an economy based on four million homeless
people, an educational network that is now entered through metal detectors,
and churches that isolate lonely-for-God members in their own subjec-tivi-
ties."[4] Even hippies of the 1960s, now entrepreneurs and corporate execu-
tives, wonder why baby busters and Gen Xers lack institutional confidence
and initiative to invest themselves in these systems gone awry.

Like children finding out that Santa Claus is not who they thought he
was, we have become disillusioned by the promises of modernity. The
vows of the Age of Reason collapse before our eyes.

The Enlightenment heralded the unlimited scope of the human spirit.
Rationalism would lead to complete knowledge. Empirical observation and
the scientific method would free us from learning based on myths and su-
perstitions, whether they were cultural or religious. Reason emerged as the
god of the human conscience. Objectivity became the hallmark of intellectual endeavor. History moved on a teleological path of unending progress.
Yet something went wrong. Oden speaks of the "enchantment of modernity," characterized by "technological messianism, enlightenment idealism,
quantifying empiricism, and the smug fantasy of inevitable historical
progress."[5] Modernism teeters on thin ice.

Standing in the wings waits a postmodern world, highly skeptical of
modernism's lost innocence and, as rapidly as it can, shedding itself of any
vestiges of a modernist worldview. What then does the postmodern landscape look like? What are some of its geographical characteristics?

The Collapse of Oz

The postmodern world appears less likely to be seduced by technology's promises. A massive economic depression sandwiched between two world wars foiled the progress modern people expected technology to bring. The most formidable weaponry ever produced by humankind still haunts the global village long after the Cold War has thawed. Though we can produce enough food for every woman, man and child on the face of the earth, people starve daily in a loveless, technological world. Technology has not rid the world of evil that breeds in the depths of human hearts. Somehow modern people thought it would.

From the coming of the automatic washing machine to the proliferation of microwave ovens, technology guaranteed us a better life by *saving us time.* We thought if we could develop machines to accomplish chores we had done by hand, the time saved could be used for intellectual pursuits (trips to the library and museums, an evening course at a local college), for recreational activities (camping, fishing, hiking, enjoying nature), for family fun (picnics in the park, playing ball with the kids). What happened? Everyone has washing machines, clothes dryers, dishwashers, ice-dispensing refrigerators, microwave ovens, garbage disposals, trash compactors, hair dryers, self-propelled lawn mowers, telephone answering machines, access to the information superhighway. Everyone has all these things, but no one has any time. We thought the gadgets we love so much would give us more time. Postmodernists strive not to be duped by such naive promises.

No one would argue with the statement that advances in medical technology have enhanced life, both quantitatively and qualitatively. People live longer, more productive lives. Each year heart bypass surgery saves thousands of lives that would have been lost to heart attacks in an earlier age. Advances in transplant techniques have freed countless patients from the weekly drudgery of kidney dialysis. Because of these wonderful— could one even classify them as miraculous?—advances in technology, modern people hoodwinked themselves into an ill-fated conviction that science and technology could accomplish virtually anything on humanity's behalf. In Oden's words, technology took on messianic proportions.

Then came the rude, frightening awakening. The AIDS epidemic has proved impervious to modern medical technology. The human immunodeficiency virus (HIV) mutates quickly, evading scientists' efforts to quell the disease. Once-well-controlled bacteria have developed their own immunity to antibiotic drugs. Deadly flesh-eating viruses stun the medical community. Pandora's box appears open, and the technological messiah remains at a loss.

Modernity scratches its bewildered head as postmodernity pulls back the curtain to expose Oz's all-too-human wizard. Yet a paradox is operating here, for postmodernism will not abandon technology. The Internet, with its ability to transport human inhabitants to cyberspace with the promise of enriching the global community, is a product of postmodern technology. Still, technology will no longer remain the panacea for society's problems. Postmodernists claim they understand technology's rightful place within our societal structure. Only time will tell if postmodernism can avoid its seductive claims.

What I See Is What I See

Postmodernism also applauds the end of modernism's love affair with objectivity and reason as the sole arbiters of truth. The modern world emerged in reaction to the medieval world, surrounded as it was with superstition and wary of any knowledge that the Roman Church did not sanction. The Enlightenment burst onto the scene with liberating energy. People could now observe, study, handle and understand the world reasonably. The human mind, illuminated by reason, could make sense out of the world objectively—for what is real is what one can see, touch, hold, sensorially experience and empirically measure.

Perhaps the greatest evidence of the shift from the medieval to the modern worldview can be seen if we trace changes in art from the Middle Ages to the modern period. While studying the shift, someone has insightfully asked, "Where are the angels?" Medieval art was awash with angels. But not so the canvases of enlightened artists. To the enlightened mind, angels were products of subjective minds attempting to make sense of a dark and unknown world. The Enlightenment changed all that, or so it thought. Art now focused on what was real. Its subjects became real farms in real countrysides dotted with real animals and earthy people. Colors were vivid and lifelike. Perspective was developed to a science. Lines were crisp and defined. The world observed was frozen in art.

If the Age of Reason could free art from the excesses of medieval myth, could it not also free other realms? Medieval religion—steeped in mystery, suffused with the miraculous, overcome with superstition—made no sense, rationally, to an enlightened worldview. To the rational mind, religion was the epitome of subjectivity. Appealing to revelation as a basis for the knowledge of God was irrational. Faith was a subjective interpretation that had no observable basis or foundation. Sensory experiences, observed and verifiable, and objective reason were the only legitimate bases for human knowledge. The heart of the modern world was formed.

Postmodernism looks askance at such objective notions of reality. Human reason represents an approach for gaining knowledge about the world in which we live. We would presume that observation of a physical phenomenon can yield something. However, because one's personal experience can color one's reasoning, postmodernists question whether pure objective reason even exists. Postmodernism remains skeptical that mere objective observation can yield anything, let alone truth. Sense data are highly subjective. What one person sees may not be what another person sees. What one person experiences in a given sensory environment may not be what another person experiences under the same conditions. Therefore, in the postmodern worldview, pure objectivity resides as a myth.

Therefore the postmodern world remains open to multifarious understandings of reality, highly skeptical of any objectified truth. In fact, the notion of absolute truth becomes oxymoronic in the pluralized epoch of postmodernism. Matters of truth are relative. It all depends on whom you ask, suggests the postmodernist. In matters of religion, philosophy or morals, one system's viewpoint offers as much validity as another's; one person's opinion is as sound as another's. Oden laments that postmodern-ism's values and source of meanings are "arbitrarily contingent upon the changing social and psychological determinants of human cultures."[6] Carl F. H. Henry bemoans that some postmodernists go so far as to claim that "objective truth is inaccessible and that meaning resides not in external reality or texts but in the interpreter."[7]

If postmodernism is right, the church has much explaining to do; if postmodernism is wrong, the church has much explaining to do. And in case you haven't noticed, angels are back!

Have It Your Way

Another defining characteristic of postmodernism is the proliferation of choices and options in every realm of life. From fast-food menus to the myriad options available for family cars or a particular kind of health insurance, we live inundated by choices. Postmodernists view this abundance of choices as needed and liberating. Plurality of interests demands plurality of choices—an expectation that ultimately colors the society's mindset when it comes to matters of religious preference.

During the modern era, people attended the church of their particular denominational heritage. Postmodern people shop for a church that offers choices. Denominational heritage quickly moves toward extinction. People want a variety of worship and program options. They also expect a variety of truth options. If the cross of Christianity is too gruesome, they can choose the pacifism of the Buddha. To them, one religious choice is as good as another. "It doesn't really matter what you believe as long as you believe something" becomes the mantra of postmodern seekers.

It's a Wonderful Day in the Neighborhood

We are witnessing the decline of rampant individualism, which also had its birth in the Enlightenment world. Descartes's "I think, therefore I am" is often cited as the intellectual moment of discovery that led to individualistic focus. In *Habits of the Heart* Robert Bellah and colleagues more than adequately described the individualism overwhelming modern culture.[8] Postmodernism calls for the resurgence of community. A recapturing of communal spirit may be on the horizon.

Perhaps an indirect point of evidence for this movement is the popularity of politically correct speech. Many scholars point to language study and usage as critical to understanding the postmodern world. Is not harmony within the community an important motivating factor in the quest for politically correct speech? Whether it's a resurgence of actual local communities or the development of virtual communities via cyberspace, the postmodern world has a communal urge. It should not go unnoticed here that perhaps no institution has more built-in resources to speak to this communal longing than the church.

"I Doubt, Therefore I Am"

Postmodernism approaches life with a hermeneutic of suspicion. People believe they have been taken advantage of. They feel their bosses at work take advantage of them. They feel merchants take advantage of them. They feel the government takes advantage of them. After a while, a paranoia brews that becomes pathological. No one is beyond suspicion. A motorist appears helpless, standing beside a car on an expressway. Steam escapes from under the raised hood. In an earlier day we would have stopped. But today who's to say it's not a ploy to ambush some unsuspecting do-gooder? We drive by, assuming the authorities will eventually come and will have the means to handle the situation.

It is ironic that the mindset that desires community becomes so suspicious that building community becomes virtually impossible. Again, does this reality offer the church a ray of hope for entering this strange new world?

The love/hate relationship with technology, skepticism about objectivity, preoccupation with choices, concern for unified communities and hermeneutic of suspicion are a few of the more salient aspects of postmodernism. The list is hardly exhaustive.

In some ways postmodernism is analogous to the theological view of realized eschatology, where the eschaton is understood as both here and yet
to come. Postmodernism represents a reaction against modernism, an end
of an era, and the beginning of something new on the horizon. It is already
here, and yet it is to come. It is an epoch in the making, one in which the
church has to live.

Apologizing for God

I began by declaring that we live and preach between times. Only a pulpit
that identifies with the milieu of the time will be heard over the babble of
other voices demanding people's attention. My earlier work on identification and preaching makes clear that identifying with the postmodern world
does not mean prima facie acceptance or rejection of its values or worldview. Creating identification means taking the postmodern world seriously
and addressing it from a collaborative rather than adversarial stance. A
postmodern world demands a pulpit willing to be a viable conversation
partner. In the words of one evangelical scholar, "The challenge for the
church is to claim this postmodern context for Christ."[9] Preaching that recognizes and addresses the shifting idioms offers the world timeless good
news of God's grace, love and provision.

The need to deal with shifting idioms became very concrete for me
when I spent two weeks teaching preaching at the Moscow Theological In-
stitute in Russia. Twenty-five pastors from across Russia's expansive land
came for two weeks of intensive training in evangelism, systematic theology and preaching. They were enthusiastic about learning Western preaching models. What primarily intrigued them was the openness of Western
pulpits. During the communist years they had, as it were, to *preach between the lines*. Like John's Revelation their sermons had to be couched in
terms that the communist leaders would not view as threatening. Now that
communism had fallen and there was a new climate of freedom, they wanted to preach an unhindered gospel. Their hearers, however, were not al-

ways sure how they should understand what they heard. *Are preachers still preaching "between the lines," or can we take what we hear at face value?* Here existed a shifting idiom those Russian pastors had to consider in order to preach effectively in their context.

Likewise, we must consider the postmodern idiom if our preaching is to gain a hearing. The modern pulpit was steeped in a reasoned homiletic, marked by point-making sermons, alliterated outlines and a third-person descriptive logic. Sermons of the modern era often talked about God, about the Bible, about life, viewing these matters like specimens under a microscope. This pulpit philosophy, saturated with rationalism, focused on factual knowledge as the sole medium for communicating religious truth. More than a few sermons addressed such issues as the location of Noah's ark and possible ways to describe the fish big enough to swallow Jonah—with the sole purpose of proving rationally the veracity of the biblical accounts. A strange venture indeed by those who claimed total reliance on the Bible but whose sermonic actions raised doubt about the text's veracity because its claims had to be empirically verified. An odd mix, when one considers the Bible's own affirmation: "For by grace you have been saved through *faith*" (Eph 2:8), and "Now *faith* is the assurance of things hoped for, the conviction of things not seen" (Heb 11:1). For modern pulpits, faith often became unwittingly a synonym for rationalism. In Tom Long's estimation we thought we were the children of Abraham but discovered we were merely the children of Descartes.

Preaching to a postmodern epoch must shed such vestiges of rationalism and take seriously the intersection between idioms of the age and the theological verities of Christian faith. "A postmodern evangelical theology," suggests Stanley Grenz, "must be post-rational."[10] Alister McGrath says, "When it comes to the big things of life—like believing in the Christian faith or believing in democracy—we live on the basis of probability, not certainty. . . . Christian faith is a risk because it cannot be proven."[11] David Buttrick asserts that what has changed in this postmodern worldview is the whole notion of reality: "Reality is less boxed in because it is no longer defined by its objective 'thereness.' No, the reality of any scene will not only be sights and sounds that can be recorded in some objective fashion, but realities in consciousness—sights, sounds, feeling, daydreams, past memories, future anticipations, fantasies, desirings, social symbols, hoary myths, and so forth."[12]

The postmodern age is an image-rich age; therefore postmodern preachers should draw on image-rich narratives and stories to present the gospel and make it clear. We do not merely tell stories for stories' sake; rather, the imagery and symbolism involved in narrative will capture postmodern imaginations and penetrate postmodern hearts. In this way preaching may gain a hearing among postmodern ears for which an earlier, rational homiletic could only wish.

A brave new world, one never envisioned by Aldous Huxley, awaits the pulpit. Is it possible to preach mystery in an age of information, hope in an era of skepticism, confidence in a time of doubt, truth in a climate of relativism? The ultimate question becomes, can we preach Christ in a postmodern world? My answer, of course, is *yes.* My suggestion is that it's time to apologize for God.

Far too many pulpits have been, for too long, apologizing—that is, making excuses—for God. Timid sermons that dismiss the sticky issues of Christian faith, sermons that water down the demands of the gospel, pabulum preaching pleasing to people's ears but unable to offer transformed lives will be transparent to the skeptical lenses of postmodernity. Will Willimon is right: the gospel of Jesus Christ is an intrusive word. It cuts against the grain of societal wisdom. It calls into question rational sensibilities and sticks its finger in the face of rabid relativism. It demands more than intellectual assent. It does not tolerate dilution in the company of modernism, postmodernism or postpostmodernism. More than anything, the postmodern world expects authenticity. If our preaching offers anything less, for God's sake let us shut up and let the stones themselves cry out.

Apologizing for God means *apologizing* for God, not *making apologies* for God. In other words, it means making a case for the gospel in all its scandalous reality. Apologizing for God means rightfully reclaiming the apologetic role of the pulpit for the cause of Christian faith. The author of 1 Peter reminded the diasporan readers, "Always be ready to make your defense to anyone who demands from you an accounting for the hope that is in you; yet do it with gentleness and reverence" (1 Pet 3:15).

The Renaissance of Apologetic Preaching

Christian apologetics begins in the Bible. The Gospels and Hebrews offered an apologetic to Jewish people about the veracity of the Christ. Paul offered a Christian apologetic to the learned Areopagus at Mars Hill. Here theology was presented in the light of a particular cultural idiom, and the gospel was preached as a viable conversation partner within that milieu. Christian communities were attacked first by Jewish leaders, then the Romans, then philosophers and politicians. All the while, the church responded by offering a defense, an *apologia*, for the faith.

As the Christian faith developed and new strands of Christian expression emerged, there was, again and again, the need to clarify and to straighten out misunderstandings of the faith, from both inside and outside the community. And thus apologetics flourished. Throughout history, Christian writers from Justin Martyr to Augustine to C. S. Lewis have defended the faith and have made a case for Christianity against the challenges of its staunchest critics and opponents. Bernard Ramm, in *Varieties of Christian Apologetics*, called apologetics "the strategy of setting forth the truthfulness of the Christian faith and its right to the claim of the knowledge of God."[13] In an era when many view Christianity as an antiquated religious option, unable to address the dilemmas of postmodern living, perhaps it's time for Christian apologetics to flourish again.

In a seminar I participated in one year at Vanderbilt University Divinity School, we pondered some key questions for theologians—particularly preaching theologians—to consider: Why did apologetics stop around the midpoint of the twentieth century? How do we do apologetics when no one cares? How do we address our generation with the gospel? How do we present what we believe as followers of Jesus Christ? How do we preach in the midst of epochal change? These questions lie at the heart of the need for apologetic preaching.

David Buttrick, who led the seminar, offered his assessment of the situation: Mainline religion is into self-preservation; American Protestantism has become hypercautious, which has led to extreme lethargy and sermons that can only be called boring. This institutional self-preservation has led to an atmosphere of doubt; people assume the church is merely speaking out of something it has at stake. Postmodern people are skeptical of such agendas. They view the church's preaching as a marketing strategy to maintain the institution, a goal for which they have little interest or energy. McGrath notes, "The institution of the church and the Christian faith itself are very easily amalgamated in people's minds. The failings of the church thus come to be projected onto Christianity itself."[14]

Apologetic preaching must offer the Christian faith without attempting to sell the church. People today have lost a sense of the presence of God; too often preachers tend to peddle the church as a substitute. The pulpit must learn to proclaim Christ while being a loyal critic of institutional religion, whether in its liberal or conservative expressions. "We are witnesses to grace, not to institutional success stories," asserts Buttrick.

We can no longer assume our preaching takes place within a more or less "Christian" culture. The great narratives of Judeo-Christian belief, the pivotal stories of the Bible's characters, the events of the life and ministry of Jesus Christ either are not known or do not carry the meaning-making significance they did for previous generations. Biblical knowledge, Christian doctrine and theological reflection must be presented and re-presented from America's pulpits—yes, even to American Christians.

Apologetic preaching presents an authentic picture of Christian faith. Apologetic preaching clarifies the misunderstandings postmodern people have about Christianity. Perhaps most important, apologetic preaching will make clear where the gospel and politically correct religious forms part ways.

The Texture and Timbre of Apologetic Preaching

Christian apologetics should have two immediate goals: (1) to present unbelievers with a viable understanding of Christian faith so they may want to make it theirs, and (2) to instruct, confirm and affirm those who are already believers in the faith. McGrath cogently addresses the situation:

> The problem is not simply how to make the Christian faith credible to the world, but for Christians to live consistently and coherently under their own claims of love and justice. This is not a matter of the world setting the church's agenda, but of the church fulfilling its own. For the church to be the church it must be concerned to transform as much of this world, after the likeness of the homeland, as it possibly can.[15]

I like the way Thomas Oden makes the point, fashioning what I would term a good apologetic for apologetic preaching:

> We have learned in modernity to keep fashionably silent about the incarnation, atonement and resurrection and to develop theological positions less controversial and more agreeable with the assumptions of modernity—that Jesus is a good teacher (with minimum "mythological" additions), that God is good, but would not dare to judge our iniquities, and so on. In only one century of focusing on the ethical relevance of Jesus' teaching, we have almost forgotten how to speak of and pray to Jesus Christ, the Son of God and Savior of the world. In the well-intentioned attempt to deliver the Christian message in a language acceptable to moderns, we have peeled the onion almost down to nothing. We have cheated our young people out of the hard but necessary Christian word about human sin and divine redemption.[16]

By its very nature apologetic preaching requires ministers to reclaim the mantle of *theologian* for the church. The demise of the apologetic voice from American pulpits suggests a dangerous trend among ministers, primarily pastors. Whether by intentional design or by default we pastors have relegated our task of being a theologian to some unknown entity while we spend our energy on matters that someone else in the church could better handle. In other words, too many pastors spend their time organizing vaca-

tion Bible school while neglecting Karl Barth. Too many ministers aspire to
be better managers of church programs. Many pastors have their hands in
every administrative pot in the church. Every committee action must have
their stamp of approval. These pastors micromanage everything from the
church's budget to Wednesday night suppers to the selection of wallpaper
for the nursery. No wonder churches languish from theological malnutri-
tion. The one charged with feeding them persists in obsessing over matters
that they could delegate to abler hands.

The early church faced a similar dilemma. Certain Hellenists com-
plained against the Hebrews because their widows were being neglected in
the daily distribution of food. The apostles called the community together
and said, "It is not right that we should neglect the word of God in order to
wait on tables. Therefore . . . select from among yourselves seven men of
good standing, full of the Spirit and of wisdom, whom we may appoint to
this task, while we, for our part, will devote ourselves to prayer and to serving the word" (Acts 6:2–4).

Apologetic preaching requires ministers to be servants of the Word. To
neglect this theological task ranks paramount to ministerial malpractice and
should not be tolerated by churches. The preacher's ideal role resides in
meaning giving. Apologetic preaching helps people to grasp the world
theologically, to bring theological meaning and understanding to their
lives. Sociologists characterize the world socially; psychologists describe
human motivation and behavior; philosophers tell us how we know; managers organize our work places; economists track our consumption of
goods and services. But theologians view the world *Godward*—that is, in
terms of relationship with God and God's ways and purposes. Apologetic
preaching offers theological meaning to a culture that desperately seeks
significance but does not know where to turn to find it.

Apologetic preaching provides people with a theological vocabulary.
Thomas Long recognizes that everyday language and speech often fail
when we try to make deeper, ultimate sense of our world. Giving congregations a theological vocabulary does not mean preaching sermons saturated

with technical terms. Some preachers even hide behind such words to conceal their own inadequacy of theological understanding. We should offer people ways of experiencing their world theologically by reclaiming the real meaning of words like *hope, faith, redemption* and *reconciliation.* Even the word *sin* can be affirmed to help people describe the ever-real presence of evil—individual, corporate, institutional—in the world.

Apologetic preaching takes seriously the mystery present at the heart of Christian faith. Though talk of mystery contradicts modernism's scientific mindset—a culture willing and able to explain everything—postmodernism, with its objective skepticism, will be open to such discussions. Stanley Grenz suggests that evangelical theology must "give place to the concept of 'mystery'—not as an irrational aspect alongside the rational, but as a reminder of the fundamentally nonrational or suprarational reality of God."[17] Given the glibness of many preachers who chirp "Jesus is the answer" without fully comprehending the depth or breadth of the question, apologetic preaching's willingness to invoke a sense of mystery serves as a needed corrective. Barth, in his *Evangelical Theology,* called Christians to a renewed sense of wonder when speaking of God. Apologetic preaching offers the opportunity for such proclamation.[18]

Apologetic preaching must be open to new paradigms of homiletic method. Modernism so binds some contemporary apologists that they exclusively use Aristotelian logic, steeped in deductive reasoning, which tilts their hand toward Western thought and exclusively Western philosophical models.[19] The postmodern worldview transcends any particular logical mode or model of reasoning. Apologetic preaching should broaden homiletic forms to include both deductive and inductive approaches, narrative as well as propositional styles, both *didache* and kerygmatic goals. For the apostle Paul no one method of proclamation held sacred status; the particular preaching situation dictated his homiletic form without any compromise of the essence of the gospel.

Apologetic preaching unashamedly takes on rival meaning systems and helps address obstacles to faith. The smorgasbord of religious options open to postmodernists rivals the array at any cafeteria. Other religious systems—Islam, New Age, varieties of Eastern cultic religions—unapologetically vie for postmodern peoples' attention and allegiance. Apologetic preaching equips Christians, intellectually and spiritually, to intelligently present and defend the Christian faith. It gives people the means to address questions of theodicy, sin, salvation in Christ, which when misunderstood become obstacles to faith.

McGrath rightly asserts, "You cannot argue people into the kingdom of God. Apologetics creates a climate favorable to faith; it does not create faith."[20] The apostle Peter warns against presenting Christianity in confrontational ways: "Always be ready to make your defense to anyone who demands from you an accounting for the hope that is in you; yet do it with gentleness and reverence" (1 Pet 3:15–16). *Gentleness* and *reverence* are the operative words for Peter. They should be the operative words for apologetic preaching.

Can we preach Christ to a postmodern world? My answer, again, is *yes.* But then again, what do I know?

2

Proclaiming Mystery in an Age of Information

T HE AGE OF INFORMATION" MIGHT BE THE MOST APPROPRIATE designation for postmodernism. Computers sit in virtually every American home waiting to whisk inhabitants into cyberspace. With the swipe of a mouse and the click of a button, one can read the latest headlines, make travel reservations, download an article from an encyclopedia, shop for a car, scan the NASDAQ or tap into major research libraries. The Internet has put immeasurable amounts of information at our fingertips—so much information that we could be called a generation of information junkies.

Recently I needed some information about a piece of software my wife had given me for my birthday. Using a popular web search engine, I entered the name of the software, hit the search key, and in less than a minute was presented with no fewer than seventy-two web sites that contained information about the software. Every site had links to other sites. Every subsequent site had links to still others, and so on. No telling how far into cyberspace I could have gone jumping from hyperlink to hyperlink. In this virtual-reality world, information appears infinite. Information is big business. But I'm not sure I want to be that informed.

High-tech information sources are not the only way contemporary culture inundates itself with information. A popular approach to marketing in recent years is the thirty-minute "infomercial." We sit before our TV screens mesmerized by the best-looking abs on the planet or by actors torching a car's fender only to find that the piece of metal, protected by a car-wax product, still holds its polished sheen. I hate watching thirty-second commercials that interrupt my favorite TV program; why would I want to sit through a thirty-*minute* commercial? Good question. But thousands of Americans must be watching, because infomercials seem to be on the increase, according to my channel-surfing survey.

A paradox seems to be operating here. While we are information overloaded, the question comes, what is the value of so much information, and for what purposes are we gathering it? It could be argued that little useful knowledge is the outcome of all the information we receive. Whether we are browsing the World Wide Web or passively watching television, information comes at us in large quantities yet with little or no time for reflection, evaluation or analysis. One can't help wondering what effect this noncritical approach to the subject matter we see and hear has on our society.

CNN's *Headline News* approach to presenting news from around the world every thirty minutes might be symptomatic of the problem. In a span of less than thirty minutes we move from a world crisis in Ethiopia to congressional hearings on the immediate topic plaguing Washington, D.C., to the latest fashions to the Hollywood minute to the sports "play of the day." Fact and fiction are interwoven at breakneck speed. Turner Broadcasting Company has obviously tapped into a market niche. The headline news format appears to be an extremely popular one compared to, let's say, *The NewsHour with Jim Lehrer* on PBS. On this program three or four news stories are dealt with in depth, reflectively and analytically. Were it not for public broadcasting, *The NewsHour* would not exist. Network television is unwilling to provide this kind of weighty coverage because, we, the consumers, won't stand for it—the ratings drop.

Despite what I have described as information overload, we still seem to be absorbed by the desire to know even more stuff than we already know. Our culture has a fascination—I could actually describe it as an addiction—with information conferences and seminars. Management seminars on dealing with difficult people, parenting seminars, pastoral leadership seminars, church-growth conferences, evangelism conferences—we're addicted. A deluge of such invitations crosses my desk weekly. One recent brochure described the "Worldwide Lessons in Leadership Series," featuring leadership gurus Stephen Covey, author of *The Seven Habits of Highly Effective People*; Tom Peters, who wrote *The Pursuit of Wow*; and Peter Senge, author of *The Fifth Discipline: The Art and Practice of the Learning Organization*. This teleconference was broadcast via satellite to more than 250 sites around the world.

There appears to be an unquenchable thirst to know more things and yet an inability to make changes with the knowledge we gain. Our jobs remain the same; our families remain the same; our communities remain the same. Then along comes another conference invitation, and off we go again.

I know a married couple who attend every marriage enrichment seminar they can fit into their busy schedules. As a matter of fact, their schedules wouldn't be so busy if they weren't killing themselves to get to the next enrichment opportunity. If frequent flyer miles were given for attending such classes, these two could travel around the world several times on the accumulated miles.

Information has become like the fix for the heroin addict. We believe if we can just get more info, we'll be better people. Yet it's hard to find time to put into practice any new insights we've gathered because we're always planning which conference to attend next. We have the misguided concept—an outgrowth of the Enlightenment—that gaining information will placate some unrelenting inner craving. Is there a cultural catharsis that comes when we attend the latest seminar? Must be!

Perhaps the compulsion for so much information is actually a compulsion to *understand* everything there is to be *understood*. For to understand is to control, to control is power, and power is ultimately the quintessential human motivation. The mindset seems to be that understanding is based on information. The corollary seems to be that ignorance means a lack of information. If we increase information, understanding will be the natural outgrowth. Yet in an information-craving, overloaded society, what is really being understood? Is it possible that the drive for understanding is also a cry for *meaning*? People appear so unsatisfied with their lives. What is wrong? Information has not touched their souls' longing for significance.

In the modern worldview, science was a god. In postmodernity, society no longer puts uncritical faith in science. People look for something else to give some significance to their existence. A significant postmodern emphasis is the pursuit of transcendence. Today people desire something beyond the mundane. People long for spiritual experiences that break them out of their routines.

Tony Campolo, speaking at a meeting of the Kentucky Baptist Convention, said, "The church will be ready for postmodernity if it rediscovers the truth it had in premodernity. It is the absurdity and foolishness of Jesus Christ."[1] For the church to return to—or to reclaim—our "absurd" roots, we will have to rethink both the *what* and the *how* of our faith. Postmodern people have not grown up in a culture permeated by Judeo-Christian values. We will have to show how the gospel of Jesus Christ answers the ultimate questions being asked by postmoderns. Christianity must show postmodern people that it speaks to their innate desire for transcendence.

Karl Barth, in *Evangelical Theology*, called for a renaissance of the sense of wonder.[2] Technology is ubiquitous in the contemporary West and has seemingly given us the wherewithal to explain our lives—from the heart of an atom to the vastness of the universe. Can we still see a rose in bloom and experience awe? Or can we describe the multiple hues of a sunset with words like *breathtaking* because our breath was literally stopped by the sunset's beauty? Wonder is wrapped up not in mere intellectual grasping of phenomena but in the realization that we are in the presence of something not quite explainable—ah, *mystery*!

Here we see the paradox of the postmodern situation. We rely on the marvels of technology. But we profoundly need the beauty of the blooming rose and relish the hues of a breathtaking sunset. Postmodernism, saturated in scientific and technological matters, is driving us to crave the simpler things that ultimately make us who we are as human beings. A sunset reminds us of a universe bigger than ourselves, beyond ourselves. *Ah, transcendence. Ah, mystery!*

Stanley Grenz suggests that evangelical theology must be postrational to affect a postmodern world. A postrational evangelical theology recognizes that the Christian faith is saturated with mystery. Essentially, the Christian faith cannot be explained rationally. This chapter discusses the dilemmas and possibilities for offering transcendence to information-overloaded people.

The Wonder and Mystery of Our Faith

The writer of the book of Hebrews reminds us that "faith is the assurance of things hoped for, the conviction of things not seen" (Heb 11:1). So from the beginning we must admit that when we talk about matters of God and faith, some things are beyond our finite comprehension and understanding. That does not mean we believe out of ignorance or live in darkness. Our understanding is based on faith. And our faith is suffused with wonder and mystery.

Apologists often attempt at this point to describe the mysteries of Christianity in terms of philosophical categories. They develop the classical proofs for the existence of God, such as the argument from efficient causality, the ontological argument or the moral argument. These arguments require deductive logic to reason their case for the existence of God, the problem of evil, the divinity of Christ or the veracity of the Bible. But as I have already noted, postmoderns are not only skeptical about religion but also skeptical—or simply apathetic—about coming to conclusions through the use of deductive logic systems. Remember, in an age of relativism even modes of proof remain in the individual mind. Hence when we describe the mysteries of Christian faith in philosophical categories that postmoderns dismiss as invalid in the first place, they will naturally respond by throwing out the faith's baby with the *philosophical system's* bath water.

In my opinion philosophical systems and rational arguments—valid as they may be for philosophers for characterizing reality and describing how we know what we know—will not win the battle for people's hearts when it comes to matters of mystery and faith. Apologetic preaching has as its purpose to make a clear defense for the faith using methods that people will not dismiss out of hand as mere sophistry.

C. S. Lewis articulates cogently the difference between how scientists describe atoms and how faith must be apprehended:

> What they [scientists] do when they want to explain the atom, or something of that sort, is to give you a description out of which you can make a mental picture. But then they warn you that this picture is not what the scientists actually believe. What the scientists believe is a mathematical formula. The pictures are there only to help you understand the formula. They are not really true in the way the formula is; they do not give you the real thing, but only something more or less like it. They are only meant to help, and if they do not help, you can drop them. The thing itself cannot be pictured, it can only be expressed mathematically. We are in the same boat here. We believe that the death of Christ is just that point in history at which something absolutely unimaginable from the outside shows through into our own world. And if we cannot picture even the atoms of which our own world is built, of course, we are not going to be able to picture this. Indeed, if we found that we could fully understand it, that very fact would show that it is not what it professes to be—the inconceivable, the uncreated, the thing from beyond nature, striking down into nature like lightning. You may ask what good will it be to us if we do not understand it. But that is easily answered. A man can eat his dinner without understanding exactly how food nourishes him. A man can accept what Christ has done without knowing how it works: indeed, he certainly would not know how it works until he has accepted it.
>
> We are told that Christ was killed for us, that His death has washed out our sins, and that by dying, He disabled death itself. That is the formula. That is Christianity. That is what has to be believed. Any theories we build up as to

how Christ's death did all this, are, in my view, quite secondary: mere plans or diagrams to be left alone if they do not help us, and, if they do not help us, not to be confused with the thing itself. All the same, some of these theories are worth looking at.[3]

Our concern as preachers, then, is not to attempt to dispel the mystery of the Christian faith but to adequately proclaim the faith, making the best defense for the hope we have. Peter's words must continue to echo in our minds: "Always be ready to make your defense to anyone who demands from you an accounting for the hope that is in you" (1 Pet 3:15).

Postmodern Messages

People today bring with them two key presuppositions. The first is *I'm okay, you're okay*. Everyone I know wants to be liked. They want to be known as friendly. They want to be accepted. In our pluralistic society we have pushed for tolerance among genders, races and ages. We have urged people to embrace diversity and learn from the richness others bring to the conversation. We poke fun at intolerance. A colleague at Southern Seminary posted on his office door a cartoon showing a monk, sporting a well-polished halo, walking down the street reading a book. The book's title: *I'm Okay, You're a Heretic*. We recognize the foolishness of presuming that others are unorthodox, even demonic, just because they don't think and act like we do.

On the surface the notion that "I'm okay, you're okay" seems quite harmless and innocent. But the problem is that it contradicts evangelical Christianity's understanding that all persons may be okay by design but are deeply flawed in practice. More clearly stated by Paul in his apologetic letter to the church at Rome: "All have sinned and fall short of the glory of God." Here's a key point where postmoderns have trouble hearing the gospel: If everyone is okay, why do we need a Savior?

It's hard for postmoderns to hear "I'm a sinner, you're a sinner." That's what makes evangelism and apologetics—in the practical arena—difficult. Often those of us with evangelistic zeal stick our fingers in the faces of those whom we consider sinners, pointing out their sins and woeful ways, alienating them instead of developing authentic, incarnational relationships with them. I fully agree with Ed Dobson's notion that the church's energy must be spent "on redeeming the lost, not rallying against them."[4] We will never claim people for Christ with holier-than-thou attitudes.

I once heard a pastor describe the modus operandi of an ordaining council with which he was familiar. The usual questions about faith and belief would be asked. When the session was almost finished, one minister—an older man who was well respected in the presbytery—would raise his hand and say, "I have one final question."

He would then ask the candidate to look out the window. "Do you see that person over there? I want you to describe what you see, theologically."

Some candidates might respond, "I see a sinner, damned and condemned before God, in need of repentance and faith. And if that person does not repent and come to faith, he will burn in hell for eternity."

Other candidates would say something like, "I see a person created in the image and likeness of God, for whom Christ died and with whom God longs to have an eternal loving and lasting relationship."

The pastor commented that the candidates who answered the question the second way invariably made the better ministers.

Apologetic preaching must take into account the presupposition "I'm okay, you're okay," adequately presenting the reality of sin while at the same time making vivid the redemption that is available in Jesus Christ. Strategies for offering such a defense of "the hope that is in you" must be thought out carefully and carried out with love (*agapē*), which always wills the well-being of the other person.

Presupposition two is "It's all right to believe anything, as long as I believe something." Postmodernity could be called the *generation of choices*. If you're not sure about this observation, just peruse the menu of your favorite—or for that matter, your not-so-favorite—fast-food restaurant, and one sure thing you'll notice is that choices abound. We are used to shopping for cars with dizzying lists of options; we are used to restaurant menus with a vast array of culinary preferences; we are used to catalogs from which we can order a shirt or blouse in every color imaginable. No wonder people expect a variety of options when it comes to religion and matters of faith. How can Christians claim their understanding of faith is the correct one? How utterly narrow-minded. How utterly absurd. From an observational standpoint—again, relying on what they learned from the empiricism of the Enlightenment—postmoderns think religions need to get with the times. If everything else in my life is custom designed just for me, why can't my religion be custom designed too?

Here again, the sensitive apologist recognizes a need to be truthful but gentle. People can be led to understand that faith in Christ offers a unique outlook of the world, one that authentically addresses people's desire for transcendence and meaning. We must offer Jesus Christ as the unique—one and only—ultimate source and goal of meaning. Let's look at some ways we can do this in our preaching.

Preaching Mystery from Postmodern Pulpits

The following questions reflect some thoughts I have gleaned from talking with people—both young and old—about issues of life. The questions come from real experiences, pointing to contemporary realities of life and the mysteries of death. Though the questions will not address the philosopher's notion of mystery, for preachers these kinds of questions get at mystery and meaning at the heart of everyday living. They touch on some of the issues deep in the hearts of thoughtful postmodern people who are not ready either to fully accept or to reject out of hand the claims of any faith system, including Christianity.

Read the questions slowly. Allow your mind to bring into focus the faces of people you know, people who are asking these very things.

1. *Where did I come from? Did I just happen, or was I an intentional creation? Why am I here? What am I here for?* These four questions deal with a search for meaning. People want their lives to have some signifi-

cance beyond mere organic existence.

2. *How should I live? Are there any absolutes today? Should I expect someone else to accept my rules of conduct? What is right and wrong?* Many people appear frustrated by the complexities of life. The rules they were taught as children no longer seem to apply. People long for some guidance for living in confused times.

3. *How can I know that God exists? If God is good and loving, why is there evil in the world? And why doesn't God do anything about it? With so many religions in the world, how can we know which one will really lead us to God?* People today have a heightened sense of spiritual concern, though it is often based on misinformation and half-truths. They appear to want to believe in God, but God doesn't always fit their rational thought systems. They often expect God to be a mirror image of themselves.

4. *Is there life after death? Where am I going after I die?* The previous questions about meaning, values and the existence of God address life here and now. These two questions, on the other hand, probe the depths of mystery. Polls indicate Americans have traditional values about life after death. To the question "Is there a heaven?" 90 percent answered *yes.* Seventy-three percent said there was a literal hell. And 87 percent responded that they believe in the resurrection of Jesus Christ.[5] Life after death lies at the heart of Christian faith. Listen to Paul's apologetic for the resurrection in the letter to Corinth:

> If there is no resurrection of the dead, then Christ has not been raised; and if Christ has not been raised, then our proclamation has been in vain and your faith has been in vain. We are even found to be misrepresenting God, because we testified of God that he raised Christ—whom he did not raise if it is true that the dead are not raised. For if the dead are not raised, then Christ has not been raised. If Christ has not been raised, your faith is futile and you are still in your sins. Then those also who have died in Christ have perished. If for this life only we have hoped in Christ, we are of all people most to be pitied. But in fact Christ has been raised from the dead, the first fruits of those who have died. (1 Cor 15:13–20)

Apologetic sermons could be preached to address each of the above questions. The sermons later in this chapter present an apologia for the resurrection to postmodern hearers. First, I should offer a brief introduction and explanation about homiletic method.

I suggest that the argumentative approach, often used in nineteenth-century pulpits, will seldom yield effective results today. That method may work when dialogue and conversation are possible; from the pulpit, however, I propose a narrative or story-based apologetic as the homiletic model. Postmodernism responds better to subjectivity than to objectivity. Postmodern people crave stories—their story, your story, human interest stories. I may be wrong, but I think the continuing proliferation of talk shows that focus on the lives of people arises from this craving. Also, the several TV programs featuring a judge listening to the personal stories of plaintiffs and defendants have nearly become a national pastime. This longing for participation in each other's story should be a hint to preachers about the homiletic method that will most effectively communicate the gospel to postmodern hearers.

The homiletic method I propose, without being dogmatic about methodology, is based on *induction* rather than *deduction*. Deductive logic requires a predisposed commitment to a premise or proposition. The primary homiletic method of the modern era used deductive logic for presenting the gospel. An example is Billy Graham's use of the phrase "the Bible says." This phrase dominated his preaching through the mid-1980s. His assumption was that if he could prove something was biblical, he would have a better chance of convincing his hearers to respond to what they heard. I presume he believed his hearers had a predisposed commitment to the Bible as an authoritative word on matters of faith.

While Graham still uses the phrase, it is not peppered as liberally throughout his sermons today. I believe the reason is that he knows he must first move his hearers to accept the Bible as a basis for faith before they will accept or believe what it says. This was not an assumption he had to make with his modern listeners. His newer strategy addresses the postmodern milieu, and thus his sermons have become more inductive in structure and method.

Please take note here that a particular homiletic method—inductive or deductive—merely has to do with *how* the message is unpacked for the listeners. In other words, homiletic method should not affect the theological content of the sermon, only how the message is communicated. My presupposition for this book is that postmodern listeners will respond more favorably to an inductive homiletic method because of this method's starting point.

Induction begins with people's experience and moves them to an appropriate conclusion. Induction in preaching often begins with human experience and moves people to the truth of biblical revelation. The inductive method, then, does not require a prior commitment to a premise or proposition. This homiletic method leads the hearers to the theological conclusion presented in the biblical text.

Thus I am proposing that apologetic preaching to postmodern listeners be sensitive to their appreciation of stories and take seriously their desire to be led to—rather than bombarded with—theological truth. The sample sermons throughout this book attempt to highlight and exemplify the homiletic method described here. Nevertheless, I am not advocating a fixed, absolute homiletic method—such would fly in the face of postmodernism's flexibility. I am suggesting a homiletic method that intentionally takes into consideration postmodernism's craving for stories and its inherent skepticism of objective religious truth.

Proclaiming the Mystery of the Resurrection: Sermon Examples

The two sermons presented here demonstrate an approach for preaching the mystery of Christ's resurrection to postmodern hearers. The goal of the sermons is for unchurched hearers to respond positively to the message of Christ's resurrection, believing that the resurrection has transforming possibilities for their lives. These two sermons are also examples of apologetic sermons to believers. Remember, apologetic preaching will equip believers to defend their faith but will also strengthen their faith. Congregations need help in dealing with the negative aspects of postmodernism. They need encouragement in their faith so their thinking and practice do not become warped, unhealthy or sinful. This is certainly an important goal of apologetic preaching.

The first sermon is an Easter sermon. As you read the opening paragraphs, notice how it addresses, head on, real issues that define a mundane existence and keep people from experiencing meaning and transcendence. These issues include *controlling, acquiring, laboring, stress, worry, anger, hurt, resentment, frustration* and *fear.* These are issues commonly understood as products of our information age. When they are named early in the sermon, people can identify with them. The sermon will then move to show how the gospel addresses these real-life issues.

Then watch for the way the sermon explicitly highlights places where people can find meaning in Christian faith. By showing that the church is the place that handles *God's stuff,* the sermon points listeners to the places where mystery intersects with the mundane. Notice that the sermon, without demeaning postmodernism, is not afraid to address issues people face today. Some matters addressed include pluralism, relativism and spirituality.

As the sermon moves toward conclusion, notice how it identifies a first-century issue with a contemporary one. Some early Christians were beginning to question the truth of the resurrection. Postmodern people demonstrate an affinity for an afterlife but would not necessarily identify Christ's resurrection with their longing for transcendence. The sermon attempts to bridge that gap.

The sermon ends with a personal illustration, the goal being to provide a subject to the sermon's thesis. This goal takes seriously postmodernism's craving for story, immediacy and authenticity through experience. The sermon unapologetically presents the Easter story as the basis for authentic faith and meaning.

I Am What I Am

1 Corinthians 15:1–11

I'm so glad you're here this morning. There are a lot of places you could be. You could be home asleep. You could be at a restaurant eating breakfast. You could be in a park taking a walk—by yourself or with some friends. You could be at a mall. You could be in a lot of places, but you chose to be here this morning, and I'm glad.

I'm glad because this is a good place to be after you've had a typical week. In last Tuesday's *Herald-Leader* a columnist described how we spend a typical week.[6] We struggle with the outside world: "controlling, acquiring, laboring, defending." All week long we deal with "stress, worry, anger, hurt, resentment, frustration, or fear." During the week we react to the world "by reflex." During the week we make sense of the world through our "own immediate experience," a vision limited by our own point of view.

But here, we hope you're a bit removed from the mundane, the commonplace. In here we gaze toward infinity. Here we're surrounded by God's stuff, and it reminds us that there really is more to life than meets the eye. It's here that we celebrate the things of our community of faith: baptisms, weddings, births and funerals, Christmas and Easter, rites of passage and opportunities of growth and commitment. That all takes place here, so I'm glad you're here this morning.

I'm glad you're here this morning because this is a safe place to be in a world confused by pluralism and religious relativism—a culture of "anything goes" in matters of faith: "it doesn't make any difference what you believe as long as you believe something." We live in a time of paradox. Our era is marked by unbelief and skepticism yet is awash in spiritual things. So we hear about Marshall Applewhite—or "Do," as he was known by his followers—and his web page, "Heaven's Gate." People awaiting the appearance of aliens and UFOs, who see Comet Hale-Bopp as a sign of revelation. Or Neale Donald Walsch, whom readers have made number three on the *New York Times* nonfiction list with his *Conversations with God.* He claims he asks God questions and God gives him the answers, which he then writes down. Why didn't I think of that? Why do books like *Conversations with God* and *The Celestine Prophecy* sell millions of copies? Because we live in a confused culture, grappling with matters of faith and disillusioned by the faith options of their parents and generations gone by.

Listen to words written two thousand years ago by the missionary Paul to the young minister Timothy:

> Proclaim the message; be persistent whether the time is favorable or unfavorable; convince, rebuke, and encourage, with the utmost patience in teaching. For the time is coming when people will not put up with sound doctrine [teaching], but having itching ears, they will accumulate for themselves teachers to suit their own desires, and will turn away from listening to the truth and wander away to myths. (2 Tim 4:2–4)

"What goes around comes around," says the modern sage. I think he's right. So I'm glad you're here this morning to hear what the church has proclaimed on this day for two millennia. Against a background not unlike our own, some Christians were beginning to question the reality of the resurrection. So Paul restates the essentials of the gospel:

> Now I would remind you, brothers and sisters, of the good news that I proclaimed to you, which you in turn received, in which also you stand, through which also you are being saved, if you hold firmly to the message that I proclaimed to you—unless you have come to believe in vain.
>
> For I handed on to you as of first importance what I in turn had received: that Christ died for our sins in accordance with the scriptures, and that he was buried, and that he was raised on the third day in accordance with the scriptures, and that he appeared to Cephas, then to the twelve. Then he appeared to more than five hundred brothers and sisters at one time, most of whom are still alive, though some have died. Then he appeared to James, then to all the apostles. Last of all, as to one untimely born, he appeared also to me. For I am the least of the apostles, unfit to be called an apostle, because I persecuted the church of God. But by the grace of God I am what I am, and his grace toward me has not been in vain. On the contrary, I worked harder than any of them—though it was not I, but the grace of God that is with me. Whether then it was I or they, so we proclaim and so you have come to believe. (1 Cor 15:1–11)

Paul reveals that the good news of Christ's death and resurrection provides the foundation on which we stand. We sometimes get caught up in nonessential matters in the church, and we lose sight of what is foundational to our faith, namely, Christ's sacrificial death and resurrection. If only we could get our priorities right and keep them before our face.

On this faith, Paul states that by the grace of God I am what I am. Aren't we all? It was twenty years ago this month that I made a conscious decision to be a disciple of Jesus Christ. Before I met Christ, I was on the management fast track in the company I worked for. I spent so much time trying to climb the corporate ladder that I neglected the needs of my wife and family. My marriage was on the rocks. I had no safety net to catch me as I fell from the success ladder into the pits of despair. But dear friends, who were believers, saw our plight and introduced us to Jesus. And by his grace—and only his grace—we were healed. Our relationship together and with God was made new. I stand before you unashamed this morning to say, By the grace of God I am what I am.

And so I'm glad you're here this morning to be reminded "of the good news that I proclaimed to you, which you in turn received, in which also you stand, through which also you are being saved: . . . that Christ died for our sins in accordance with the scriptures, and that he was buried, and that he was raised on the third day in accordance with the scriptures, and that he appeared to [multitudes.] . . . So we proclaim and so you have come to believe." That is our faith, that is our cry.

The second sermon was preached shortly after the above Easter sermon. Again, the primary message is the impact the resurrection of Jesus Christ can have on postmodern hearers. Out of the gate the sermon confronts some contemporary attempts to debunk the resurrection as an actual event in time and space. Since the resurrection is a mystery, we must show that it cannot be explained by rationalism or the scientific method. The sermon points this out.

The sermon also shows how fear over everyday problems can cripple our thinking and our response to Christ: "Fear drove them to lock themselves up to protect their lives." Notice also how the sermon uses anecdotes, story and the biblical narrative to lead hearers to see that Christ's resurrection becomes a very real possibility for them to believe. Because postmodern people look and long for transcendence, the sermon attempts to show rather than merely explain that such is possible through faith in Jesus Christ. Even Thomas' doubt was abated. Also, like the first sermon, this sermon should help equip believers with handles for dealing with their own doubts regarding their faith and for dealing with the questions others ask about following Jesus Christ as the risen Lord and Savior.

Strange Things Happen Behind Closed Doors
John 20:19–31

A recent issue of *Newsweek* magazine included a long article on the resurrection of Jesus. Among many quotations from ministers, theologians and religious leaders, one comment caught my attention. A theologian declared that the resurrection was something that "happened to and with the disciples." Not something that happened with Jesus, but something that happened to and with the disciples. In other words, the resurrection was a faith figment of their imaginations. He argues that the resurrection occurred for them at the moment they believed. He summarized Easter this way: "To believe in the possibility of resurrection is the essence of Christianity."

The New Testament boldly and scandalously claims that the resurrection happened to Jesus—and not just to the disciples. The resurrection is not just a possibility. For two thousand years, Christians have claimed the resurrection as a historical event. As my friend Carey Newman wrote: "The resurrection demonstrates God's objective involvement in this world and should never be depicted as simply a subjective experience of Jesus' disciples, ancient or modern."

What happened on that first Easter was more than the wishful thinking of a merry band of Jesus' followers. The biblical story paints a much different picture. It was evening on Sunday, Easter Sunday. The disciples were hiding out, probably in the same room where Jesus had washed their feet, where they had shared the Passover meal together, where he had spoken about a new covenant. That was last week. Tonight they met in terror. The window shades were drawn tight. The doors of the house were barred and locked. The disciples feared repercussions from the religious leaders. The rulers had gotten to Jesus; it only made sense that in a matter of time they would be next. They listened to every footstep on the stairway. They braced at every knock on the door.

In *The Diary of Anne Frank* young Anne describes the fear she and her family felt as they hid, huddled in a small attic, from the Nazis. Every scream of Gestapo sirens sent chills of fear down their spines. They lost their breath at every knock on the front door. They lived in constant horror behind locked doors, fearing for their lives. Their fear was well founded.

Fear caused the disciples to huddle together in that room for protection. Surely they had heard the news by now—the news about the tomb being empty. Yet even the news of the empty tomb and Jesus' resurrection had not transformed their spirits. The room became a prison—fear kept them inside. Fear drove them to lock themselves up to protect their lives.

I have known some Christians who live in fear, constant dread. I'm not talking about fear of arrest or apprehension about persecution. When I taught in Moscow, several student pastors told us about palpable fear—fear they could feel while holding clandestine church services, fear they could almost touch as they lived out the gospel under the communist regime. I'm not talking about that kind of fear.

I know Christians who lock themselves behind doors of fear. Their situations are not to be taken lightly. The threat of a layoff, the loss of a job, the inability to find work because you're told you're overqualified—these are real dilemmas.

Fear about financial pressures: "How are we going to make ends meet? Whom can I pay late this month? How did we allow our debt to get so out of hand?" And the anxiety the problems trigger can be crippling.

There are people so fearful about their children's future that they become physically ill thinking about it: "What will the world be like when my baby is a teenager? What kind of world will we leave our children?" asked the young mother. "With all the violence and the immorality, I'm just so frightened about it. I just don't know what to do!"

I once spoke to a seminary student who lived in total fear of disappointing his parents. He was nearly paralyzed by the thought of having to go home at Christmas break and tell his parents he realized God was not calling him into ministry. Tearfully he asked me, "How can I face them? My great-grandfather was a preacher. My grandfather was a preacher. My father was a preacher. I have two uncles who are preachers. I'm so afraid that I will disappoint them. It will kill them. I just know it!"

What about your greatest fear? What do you most dread? What is your greatest doubt? We lock ourselves into a prison of fear and live as though the tomb still held Jesus.

Suddenly, Jesus stepped into the middle of the disciples' fear and said, "Peace be with you." The risen Lord broke into their prison to free them from fear. Jesus broke into their midst to give them his peace. "Peace be with you," Jesus said, and then he showed them his hands and his side. Then it was party time—a time for celebrating. When they saw Jesus they shouted!

Tony Campolo is right: the kingdom of God really is a party. It calls for celebration, because "in all these things we are more than conquerors through him who loved us," writes Paul in his letter to the church at Rome. "For I am convinced that neither death, nor life, nor angels, nor rulers, nor things present, nor things to come, nor powers, nor height, nor depth, nor anything else in all creation"—not our fears about jobs, or finances, or children, or doubts—"will be able to separate us from the love of God in Christ Jesus our Lord" (Rom 8:37–39).

In our fears, our confusion and our anxiety, the risen Lord stands with us. In our problems, personal or community, the risen Lord stands with us. In facing obstacles of faith and challenges of life, the risen Lord stands with us. The Lord stands among us with the peace of his presence. The risen Christ confronts us in our doubts and fears with his living presence, fortifying our faith so that we might withstand the doubt.

Jesus said to them again, "Peace be with you. As the Father has sent me, so I send you." The disciples hid behind closed doors to protect themselves from becoming victims. The resurrected Christ freed them to open the door and witness boldly concerning what they had seen and experienced. Jesus came and met them in their fear and wasted no time giving them a commission: "Just as the Father sent me, now I'm sending you." And Jesus gave them the Holy Spirit. For John, the writer of this Gospel, the resurrection, the ascension and Pentecost merge into a single event.

Do you see the urgency and irony of the moment? From fear-filled followers to fearless missionaries. It's just amazing what Jesus can do!

But there's a little more to the story. Thomas, one of the Twelve, was not with the others when Jesus came.

> The other disciples told him, "We have seen the Lord." But he said to them, "Unless I see the mark of the nails in his hands, and put my finger in the mark of the nails and my hand in his side, I will not believe." (Jn 20:24–25)

Most of the disciples had been trapped in fear. Thomas was ensnared in doubt. Thomas withdrew from fellowship. He sought loneliness rather than togetherness. Because he was not with the others, he missed the first coming of Jesus.

When sorrow comes and sadness surrounds us, we often shut ourselves up and refuse to be with people. That is the very time when, in spite of our sorrow, we should seek the fellowship of Christ's people, for it is there that we are likeliest of all to meet him face to face.

Now a week had gone by and the disciples were again in the house. Thomas was with them this time. Just as on Easter, Jesus came and stood among them and said, "Peace be with you."

Then he said to Thomas, "Put your finger here and see my hands. Reach out your hand and put it in my side. Do not doubt but believe."

Thomas answered him, "My Lord and my God!" And Thomas's words become the hallmark for the early church. The words should become our words when we meet the risen Christ.

Jesus said to him, "You believed because you have seen me? Blessed are those who have not seen and yet have come to believe."

And John closes his Easter story by noting that Jesus did many other signs in the presence of his disciples, which John didn't write down in his Gospel. But these are written so that "you may come to believe that Jesus is the Messiah, the Son of God, and that through believing you may have life in his name."

I'm glad that theologian quoted in *Newsweek* is wrong. Without the resurrection and without Jesus, the church would have no message, no power, no one to turn to when up against difficulties. Without the resurrection, we'd better lock the doors, for we have much to fear.

Blaise Pascal, the French scientist, mathematician and philosopher, was working at his laboratory shortly after his beloved daughter had died. A friend dropped by and was amazed by Pascal's sense of peace in the face of tragedy. The friend said, "I wish I had your creed; then I would live your life."

Pascal countered: "Live my life and you will soon have my creed." The faith that frees us is real, practical and experiential.

Don't be afraid. Be free. Be free. He is alive! He is risen!

In Summary

This chapter addressed the question, *Is it possible to preach mystery in an age of information*? It addressed the dilemmas of and possibilities for offering transcendence to information-overloaded people. By its nature, postmodernism pursues and readily embraces transcendence, while at the same time it is marked by a flood of information. This chapter showed how our preaching can unravel and respond to the mystery-information paradox of postmodernism. Our preaching should capitalize on that paradox as a way to appeal to and connect with those affected by postmodernism.

In the next chapter we turn our attention to another challenge for us as preachers: proclaiming hope in an era of skepticism.

3

Proclaiming Hope in an Era of Skepticism

EARLIER GENERATIONS BELIEVED IN THE INEVITABLE PROGRESS of the human spirit. Following World War II, Americans soared into the second half of the twentieth century full of energy, excitement and hope. The war years had ended; America's soldiers had returned victorious from Europe and the Far East. Propelled by the G.I. Bill, thousands of young veterans swelled the ranks of vocational schools and colleges in pursuit of a better way of life. Up to that time people had considered a college education a major luxury, an opportunity afforded to the few. Now a university education fell within reach of the masses making up America's middle class. What their parents and grandparents could only dream about, young Americans were experiencing firsthand.

Along with the educational flurry came a boom in available housing. Virtually millions of couples took advantage of low-interest Veterans Administration home mortgage loans. Subdivisions sprang up overnight as people moved from cities to suburbs, providing families a way of life that older Americans could hardly envision. With sodded lawns and transplanted trees, empty lots and acres of uninhabited farmland became paradise. Children could romp and play in backyards transformed into miniature parks. Above-ground swimming pools dotted the newly formed landscape. Subdivided parcels of land became neighborhoods; neighborhoods produced communities. Communities generated optimism. America was hopeful; Camelot had arrived.

The Fall of Camelot: Skepticism Dawns

During many epochs, the collapse of a dream remains difficult to pinpoint. Historians generally refrain from trying to name the date or even the decade when the Roman Empire fell. Its demise came gradually, a cultural and political evolution understood most clearly in hindsight.

It is difficult to pin down the point of cultural demise in many countries, but the American Camelot's downfall is easier to date. Not that the waning of American hopefulness and the advent of skepticism is on the scale of the fall of the Roman Empire. I'm merely suggesting that it is possible to date a major psychic shift in the United States.

Most Americans—dare I say most people in the modern world?—who were alive on November 22, 1963, remember exactly what they were doing that day. A month earlier, almost to the day, my family had celebrated my thirteenth birthday. That fateful November day unfolded most typically. It was early afternoon. The Pennsylvania fall was almost over. Most of the autumn foliage had fallen from the trees. The sun shone, but a sturdy breeze, crisp and clean, whispered to us that winter was not far off. We were busily taking notes in Mr. Jones's eighth-grade American history class; the immediate subject was the Battle of Gettysburg.

The principal's faltering voice over the school's PA system interrupted discussion of the battle. We stared at one another, shocked. Classmates began to cry—white classmates and black classmates; girls and boys; Jewish kids, Methodist kids, Catholic kids, Baptist kids. The news of President Kennedy's assassination took us all by surprise. As young teenagers we could not possibly measure or comprehend the impact of his death. We didn't know it, but Camelot was gone.

The sixties burst onto the world scene bringing enormous social, political and cultural changes. Around the world there were hints that the optimism of the previous decade might have been a façade. We could cite a host of ominous issues and events that brought American dreams into question. The Cold War loomed like a specter over Europe and the world. The United States and the Soviet Union expended massive amounts of capital developing weapons of mass destruction. Threat and counterthreat became the norm for international diplomacy. *Détente,* a word we had never heard before, was being used to excess. Nuclear deterrence became the theory of choice to keep the world from entering a nuclear holocaust winnable by no nation. In other words, if you build ten nuclear weapons, I'll match your ten and raise the odds by building several more. Politicians and military experts played a poker diplomacy to keep peace. Peace theory was based on a strange paradox of keeping a balance of power by always matching military might with more of the same.

The world was skeptical that anyone, even America, could avoid a war with the Soviet Union. A proliferation of bomb shelters were built in suburban homes and backyards. The neighborhoods so adored in the fifties as sanctuaries of sanity were now being fortified as possible battle zones.

My maternal grandfather, Andy Fowler, was convinced that *the Russians*—he always referred to the Soviet Union that way—would attack the United States. U.S. leaders bragged about our first-strike capability and our intention to maintain a first-strike stance. Under "first-strike theory," if things got so hot politically and militarily as to bring us to the brink of nuclear war, the United States would not wait to launch nuclear weapons until after the Soviet Union launched theirs. First strike guaranteed, in principle, that the United States would at least get its weapons into the air before the Soviet Union destroyed them on their launching pads or in their silos.

Along with fire drills, we had air raid drills at school. We would practice hiding under our wooden desks, or we ran into the hallway to shield ourselves from shattering glass. We didn't know that such attempts to protect ourselves would have been absolutely futile had we been exposed to an actual nuclear attack. Still, in the face of potential nuclear devastation the optimism of the 1950s waned. Skepticism was born. It was hard to be hopeful when the world appeared to be such a hostile place.

While we were preparing for international confrontation, American cities were erupting with the civil rights movement. Families living in the suburbs either knew nothing of or ignored the plight of African-Americans in both northern and southern cities. The civil rights movement trumpeted that there was trouble in paradise. Southern cities like Birmingham and Memphis were caldrons of social unrest preparing to boil over. Evening news reports showed riot police releasing attack dogs on bands of black demonstrators. Violent streams of high-powered water cannons blasted black men, women and children off the streets. While my classmates and I studied the Declaration of Independence and the U.S. Constitution, thousands of fellow citizens were not allowed to drink from the same water fountains or use the same restroom facilities afforded to white customers.

The civil rights movement showed that African-American citizens were skeptical that the American dream was their dream too. In 1963, when Dr. Martin Luther King Jr. spoke of having a dream, it was not only his dream but the dream of a people. One hundred years earlier Abraham Lincoln had signed the Emancipation Proclamation. Many African Americans were still doubtful that they would see authentic emancipation in their lifetime.

By the late 1960s the country was bogged down in a military/political quagmire. The Vietnam War, coming to the American conscience in earnest at the close of the decade, seemed to highlight all that was failing us as a nation. Young men burned their selective service draft cards to protest what they believed to be American aggression on the Vietnamese people. Those who felt that the United States was playing politics in matters better left to the Vietnamese people called the war evil and *immoral*. Chants like "Hell no, we won't go!" were heard on the evening news as camera crews followed "draft dodgers" to safe havens in Canada.

World War II veterans, many of them fathers of those protesting the war, could not understand how their sons could act so "unpatriotic." To those older veterans, unrestrained loyalty to God and country was the mark of patriotism. When Uncle Sam called men to serve in the armed forces, earlier generations had stepped up to the task unquestioningly. But those of military draft age in the sixties saw authentic patriotism in the willingness to challenge and protest decisions made by a government that they could not support—just another sign that Camelot had collapsed.

Because of the Cold War, the country's inability to guarantee its African-American citizens the same rights as its white citizens and America's involvement in an apparently unwinnable war in Vietnam, Americans—especially young Americans—became deeply skeptical that the government, or any institution for that matter, could make a difference in their lives. Institutions seemed inherently evil to many young people; all of them came under suspicion and were called into question.

The church, too, felt the rumblings of massive social restructuring and change. During the 1960s states began to strike down so-called blue laws—laws requiring stores and business to be closed on Sundays. Until that point Sunday had been virtually a day of rest throughout the land because you couldn't buy anything or go anywhere on Sundays.

In a tongue-in-cheek way William Willimon traces the beginning of the change to a Sunday evening in 1963 in Greenville, South Carolina.[1] Ignoring the state's blue laws, the Fox Theater opened on Sunday. Willimon and six of his friends were members of the Methodist Youth Fellowship of the Buncombe Street Church. They made a pact to enter the front door of the church, make sure they were seen, then quietly exit the back door and "join John Wayne" at the Fox Theater.

Willimon says that evening was "a watershed in the history of Christendom, South Carolina style." Their parents had never worried about whether they would grow up Christians. As in many rural towns the church was "the only show in town." On Sundays you couldn't even buy a gallon of gas, and if you ran out of milk you had to wait till Monday. There was a traffic jam on Sunday mornings at 9:45, when everyone headed for their respective Sunday schools. Willimon says, "People grew up Christian simply by being lucky enough to be born in places like Greenville."

Well, that all changed that night in 1963 when owners of the Fox Theater decided that there wasn't much wrong with seeing a movie on Sunday evening.

Perhaps that's not the best history, but it illustrates the point. Even the church's institutional stronghold on cultural values was loosened. For better or worse the world had changed. Institutions, whether the government, businesses or the church, could no longer expect absolute loyalty and allegiance. The skepticism of the age affected every realm of life, public and private.

Postmodern people, disillusioned by promises of modernity, no longer share the naive hope held out by the 1950s worldview. It's a frenetic, skeptical and sometimes cynical world. Can Christian theology respond with hope to cynical people? Is it possible for the church's proclamation to gain a hearing for hope in such a skeptical age?

The Basis of Christian Hope

For Christians the word *hope* implies more than a sappy version of wishful thinking. A high-school student who didn't study as hard as he could have might yearn for a good outcome on a final exam. A young woman might long for a positive result on a stress test she just underwent. It's overly optimistic to think that the flashing blue lights on the car behind you are merely for decoration. But such longings remain in the realm of *wishful thinking*.

Hope transcends human longing or desires. Hope remains at the center of the gospel of Jesus Christ and therefore at the center of Christian theology. The Christian faith is hope-based and hopeful. That hope grounds itself in an intrinsic relationship with God and God's action.

According to Genesis 1:26–27, God created human beings in his own image and likeness. Theologians refer to the *imago Dei*—the image of God—as that quintessential element within our humanness that separates human beings from all other forms of life. Being created in the image and likeness of God grounds hope not in human design or ingenuity or resourcefulness, or even possessions, but in God. To illustrate the point, Paul admonishes Timothy about the source of hope: "As for those who in the present age are rich, command them not to be haughty, or to set their hopes on the uncertainty of riches, but rather on God who richly provides us with everything for our enjoyment" (1 Tim 6:17). Present hope, based on God's goodness, yields all that human beings could possibly need.

With creation at its root, the Christian gospel's message remains saturated in and points ever forward to hope. The incarnation of Jesus Christ expresses God's hopefulness for reconciliation with the world. Paul's words to the Corinthian church exemplify this fact: "In Christ God was reconciling the world to himself" (2 Cor 5:19).

At first glance, the trial and crucifixion of Jesus Christ are signs of an utter, tragic devastation of hope. But the paradox of the Christian faith abides here. For within the pain and sacrificial death of Jesus Christ, ultimate and eternal hope erupts. Jesus' words "It is finished," viewed skeptically, could be understood as a submission to defeat—the powers of this world got their way. Yet taken hopefully, the words describe the culmination of God's goals for Christ's coming into the world. The Word that became flesh declares the accomplishment of his eternal destiny.

The promise of the gospel exists in hope. Paul made this extremely clear when he wrote to the Colossians of the reconciliation promised "provided that you continue securely established and steadfast in the faith, without shifting from the hope promised by the gospel that you heard, which has been proclaimed to every creature under heaven. I, Paul, became a servant of this gospel" (Col 1:23).

Christian hope is forward-looking. It looks beyond what is to what can be. I remember hearing Bobby Kennedy say, "Some people see the world the way it is and ask, 'Why?' Others see the world the way it can be and ask, 'Why not?'" Christian hope looks at the world and asks, Why not?! It begins to sense realities where only possibilities exist today. It says to a world living on shattered dreams, "Don't despair. Don't give up. Lift up your chin and look what God has done, is doing and will do." Peter understood this reality of hope when he wrote, "Therefore prepare your minds for action; discipline yourselves; set all your hope on the grace that Jesus Christ will bring you when he is revealed" (1 Pet 1:13).

Faith, hope and love are integrally entwined. Hope taken without faith is nothing more than wishful thinking. Hope and faith are products of Christian love. The three cannot be separated in a homiletic theology for the twenty-first century. Paul's incredible words recorded in 1 Corinthians 13 point to this. The writer of Hebrews likewise ties faith and hope together: "Now faith is the assurance of things hoped for, the conviction of things not seen" (Heb 11:1). Again, Paul's encouragement to the Christians in Rome points out the relationship between hope and faith: "For in hope we were saved. Now hope that is seen is not hope. For who hopes for what is seen? But if we hope for what we do not see, we wait for it with patience" (Rom 8:24–25).

The Christian faith hopes within the daily experiences of life. As noted earlier, postmoderns are increasingly interested in spiritual matters and tend to view the transcendent with less skepticism than their modern forebears. They also know that they live in the here and now. They expect any religious system to which they would give their allegiance to speak to the daily life situations they face. That's what our congregations expect from us as well. And may we be keen to realize that we, the church, are a part of the postmodern mindset. So, people ask, will your faith help me face a boss who takes advantage of me? Will your religion help me cope with teenagers who are out of control? Will your religion accept me even though I am divorced? Will your religion walk with me Monday through Friday? Or is your faith a Sunday-only proposition?

As we preach, we must strive for balance when addressing these needs. There is always the danger of reducing what should be thoughtful theological discourse—sermons—to mundane chatter that is nothing more than pop psychology baptized in Jesus talk. But we don't have to offer mundane chatter. The hope of the gospel of Jesus Christ does speak to the daily realities of postmodern living. Paul doesn't sound like a mere academic theologian when he says, "Or does he not speak entirely for our sake? It was indeed written for our sake, for whoever plows should plow in hope and whoever threshes should thresh in hope of a share in the crop" (1 Cor 9:10). Here is the Christian faith cutting into the warp and woof of daily life. Christian faith lives for today and is the bright hope for tomorrow.

While it goes without saying, it helps me to remember now and again that hope begins with and ends with and is grounded in God: "For to this end we toil and struggle, because we have our hope set on the living God, who is the Savior of all people, especially of those who believe" (1 Tim 4:10). Hope motivated the early church at Pentecost. Hope still empowers the church today.

Proclaiming Hope: Sermon Examples

The first sermon example below was preached on Pentecost Sunday. It is an apologetic sermon directed to seekers who, living in a postmodern context, find themselves rather cynical about organized religion in general. They also find that Christianity's record throughout history appears somewhat tarnished. In the sermon, keeping in mind 1 Peter 3:15–16, I tried to disarm their cynicism by confronting head-on the very issues that were getting in the way of their responding to the gospel. One strategy I used was to deal candidly with the anxieties of postmodernism, especially relativism and pluralism. Look for this strategy in the introduction of the sermon. The rhetorical question I pose was my attempt to probe these issues: "Isn't religion supposed to be a personal matter, something on which to reflect and meditate?"

Following this comes a frank discourse about the sadder side of Christian history, such as the Crusades and the Inquisition: "The Christian mission to take the gospel to the world hasn't always been very Christian." My goal is to show postmodern listeners that I am aware of valid objections they raise to the way Christians have treated others in history. This creates a level of authenticity and credibility for skeptical ears.

My strategy is then to suggest that while Christian history hasn't always been *Christian*, the primary message of the gospel is surrounded by hope. Here is the apologetic motive. As the sermon states, "Rather than salespeople trying to sell their religion, we see witnesses who draw a crowd by the content of their message." The authentic content of our message is the basis for Christian hope. Pentecost, the birthday of the church, becomes an appropriate day to celebrate and reconfigure for postmoderns, in light of their cynicism and skepticism, an authentic picture of the hope of our faith.

"What Does This Mean?"

Acts 2:1–13

I don't know how it makes you feel, but my anxiety always rises when I'm confronted by someone who's trying to sell me their religion. I can remember walking briskly through an airport, trying to catch a plane. Suddenly in the distance I heard them—the rhythmic drumbeats, the chiming ring of finger cymbals. Oh no, I thought. *Not them.* I dreaded meeting them in their saffron-colored robes and their characteristic hairstyles. I knew they'd want to give me a flower, offer me a tract, share their worldview and wish me well on my way. I really didn't need their good wishes—after all, I had my own religion.

It always makes me anxious when people try to sell me their religion. You know who I mean, don't you? Those well-meaning, zealous missionaries for some religious group, knocking at your door at the most inopportune time, telling you that all you believe, all you have based your life on when it comes to religion, is wrong. Then they have the gall to tell you they hold the truth you need. "The audacity," we mutter under our breath. "Who do they think they are?" we wonder. "No thank you!" we curtly reply. "We don't need any truth today!" As we walk away from the door, the slam still echoing in our ears, we vow never to be so offensive with our faith.

Isn't religion supposed to be a personal matter, something on which to reflect and meditate? I get nervous when people try to peddle their religion to me. That's what makes me a little uncomfortable about Pentecost. Aren't these disciples being a bit flagrant with their faith? I know they're acting on Jesus' commission to go and make disciples of all nations, baptizing them and teaching them everything he had commanded them. Pentecost marks the genesis of the Christian mission of taking the gospel to the world. I guess that's where some of my misgivings begin.

The Christian mission to take the gospel to the world hasn't always been very Christian. In fact, the church has a rather poor track record when it comes to being "a kinder, gentler" religion. Jesus taught his followers to be peacemakers. History shows that most of the church must have been absent from class that day. There have been times when the church just didn't get it.

The Crusades are a good example. When you're not getting your theological way, turn your plowshares into swords and muster an army in Jesus' name. And from the eleventh to the thirteenth centuries, that's exactly what European Christians did. "Onward Christian soldiers," bound and determined to wrest the Holy Land out of the hands of "Muslim infidels." No doubt some Christians had fallen under persecution by the Turks. But Christian zeal encouraged participation in the Crusades. It was considered an act of atonement, gaining "credit" in heaven for the crusader. So under the "banner of the cross," off they marched to present the gospel to the "heathen"—one way or another. *The Christian mission to take the gospel to the world hasn't always been very Christian.*

Then there was the Inquisition, another example of how the church just didn't get the gospel. Overall, the Inquisition was a system of tribunals aiming to seek out and prosecute heretics. Since Christianity was the established religion of the Holy Roman Empire, heresy was considered a civil and religious crime. Heretics were a threat to church and to social order. The tribunal could sentence one to death for not believing correctly or for having beliefs that didn't conform precisely to the official interpretation of church dogma. Coerced confessions of heresy were the rule rather than the exception. Witnesses—only two were needed—were often bribed by authorities to give a false report on a suspected heretic.

The inquisitors based the practice on St. Augustine's interpretation of Luke 14:23 as sanctioning the use of force against heretics. Luke 14:23 says: "Then the master said to the slave, 'Go out into the roads and lanes, and *compel* people to come in, so that my house may be filled.' " Jesus does use the word *compel,* but the compelling is to a banquet, not to the gallows. It goes to show how the Bible can be used to advance just about anyone's pet agenda. *The Inquisition is another example that the Christian mission to take the gospel to the world hasn't always been very Christian.*

Christians of every age had better be careful, because it's an easy slip from authentic Christian zeal to the Inquisition. When the word *Christian* is used to promote a politics of polarization, that should alarm us. When the word *Christian* is used to emphasize a political ideology rather than authentic spirituality, that should alarm us. When the word *Christian* is used to advance a particular brand of politics, that should alarm us. When the word *Christian* is used to champion dogmatism and intolerance, that should alarm us.

Yes, the Christian mission to take the gospel to the world hasn't always been very Christian. And Pentecost marks the birthday of the church, the genesis of the Christian mission to the world. According to the text in Acts, 120 followers of Jesus spoke languages other than their own, caused the crowd who heard them to marvel, and became the laughingstock of some who thought they were hitting the wineskins a wee early in the morning.

At first glance the whole scene probably makes us a little skeptical, especially if we get nervous when people try to peddle their religion to us. These disciples are being rather forward with their faith. So what does all this mean?

One person characterized the day of Pentecost as the church "going public." Before Jesus was taken into heaven, he said to the disciples: "You will be my witnesses in Jerusalem, in all Judea and Samaria, and to the ends of the earth" (Acts 1:8). The disciples had been staying together, keeping a low profile, wondering and waiting for God to move. When the day of Pentecost came, a sound like the rush of a violent wind "filled the entire house where they were sitting. Divided tongues, as of fire, appeared among them, and a tongue rested on each of them. All of them were filled with the Holy Spirit" and, with the Spirit's ability, "began to speak in other languages."

Will Willimon says that here "timid disciples found their tongues to proclaim the truth of Christ."[2] The story of Pentecost is problematic for those who want religion to be merely a personal matter, something on which to reflect and meditate. "Luke goes to great pains to insist that this outpouring of the Spirit is anything but interior. Everything is by wind and fire, loud talk, buzzing confusion, and public debate," Willimon insightfully suggests.[3]

Reminiscent of God's Spirit hovering over the formless earth and the chaotic waters of Genesis, preparing creation for the creative Word of God, the Spirit hovers over the church, giving the disciples the power "to 'go public' with its good news, to attract a crowd and to have something to say worth hearing."[4]

Rather than salespeople trying to sell their religion, we see witnesses who draw a crowd by the content of their message. They herald good news. Life is different now because Jesus Christ lived, died and lives again. Relationships take on new light because of the Christ event. A kingdom ethic supplants conventional wisdom, morals and ideals. How we make sense out of life, how we cope with anxiety, the way we respond in grief, the way we approach the forgotten people we pass on the street, our actions on behalf of ignored, lonely people are significantly transformed through the Holy Spirit's power. The Holy Spirit at Pentecost enabled the church to go public into the world with a witness of the gospel. There's nothing for sale here.

It's good news; it's a gift.

Today is Pentecost Sunday. Here we sit together, keeping a low profile, wondering and waiting for God to move. Yet knowing God's Spirit has already empowered us—not as hawkers of some human ideology, not as peddlers of someone's narrow political agenda, not as crusaders or heretic hunters, but as witnesses. What those disciples bore witness to in Jerusalem, we continue to bear witness to in Lexington. Pentecost marks the genesis of the Christian mission of taking the gospel to the world. Pentecost today marks the continuity of this body of believers with that mission. "You will receive power when the Holy Spirit has come upon you," Jesus said, "and you will be my witnesses to the ends of the earth."

"Witnesses," he said. That's what Pentecost is about. Witnesses—that word carries a lot of baggage in church, doesn't it? We often think of witnessing as walking up to total strangers on the street, handing them a copy of "The Four Spiritual Laws" and asking them if they're saved. That certainly is a type of witness, but that's not all there is. Jesus said, "You will be my witnesses." Witnesses are those who attest to what they have seen with their own eyes, experienced in their lives, sharing a story. We are witnesses of hope. We can say to a world that is sometimes skeptical about what they hear from religious folk, "There is hope."

Frederick Buechner, in his essay "A Sprig of Hope," retells the story of Noah and the flood. My favorite part is when he describes the return of the dove:

> After many days, Noah sent forth a dove from the ark to see if the waters had subsided from the earth, and that evening she returned, and lo, in her mouth a freshly plucked olive leaf. . . . The dove stands there with her delicate, scarlet feet on the calluses of his upturned palm. His cheek just touches her breast so that he can feel the tiny panic of her heart. His eyes are closed, the lashes watery wet. Only what he weeps with . . . is no longer anguish but wild and irrepressible hope. That is not the end of the story in Genesis, but maybe that is the end of it for most of us—just a little sprig of hope held up against the end of the world.[5]

We are witnesses of hope. Hope that comes to us when a child utters her first word. Hope that peeks in when tulips bloom and trees bud with new leaf. Hope that quietly consoles even in the presence of death. Hope that refuses to allow sin to have the last word. Hope that confronts evil with love. Just a little sprig of hope held up against the pain of the world.

We are witnesses of love. Not cheap, counterfeit love spoken to appease a guilty conscience. Not love that expresses the delight we have over a new boat or a trip to the Bahamas. But unconditional love that runs out to meet us on our return from the far country. Love that forgives our thoughtless actions. Love that has no agenda. Love not purchased. Love that sees with loving eyes.

We are witnesses of good news. People who have lost their dreams need some good news. The song "The Class of '57" captures the emotions so many people today experience. Here is a high-school class whose dreams soared to change the world, but their reality has never flown quite so high. The used-car salesman, the beautician, the truck driver, the seller of real estate—their former dreams are mocked by the mundane realities of day-to-day existence. Their lives are empty. Too many people experience life as this kind of emptiness. But we Christians are hopeful; we are witnesses of good news.

In Isaiah 65:17–25 the prophet describes the peaceable kingdom in which all life has meaning and joy. Later in the book of Acts, Luke records that day by day Jesus' followers spent time together in the temple (not just for an hour or two on Sundays). They shared meals that were characterized by gladness and generosity. They spent time together praising God. The gospel had transformed their lives. Their daily routines were dictated by the fellowship they now experienced in Christ. The poor were cared for. Injustice was challenged wherever it was found. They began to live together the way they would live eternally in God's kingdom. Isaiah's vision was erupting onto the scene.

Pentecost can do that. It's what happens when the church goes public. It's what happens when the Spirit breathes.

The second example is an apologetic sermon intended for Christians. Here I hope to strengthen their faith and enable them to more effectively deal with the hope-robbing moments in their lives. The gospel offers an apologetic appeal for those who share its claims as well.

Notice the inductive movement as the sermon begins. By sharing some personal thoughts, I attempt to bring the hearers along with me on my journey of discovery. I hope God will reveal to them through the sermon what I discovered as I studied and pondered the text. Even though I can presume that my hearers do accept my worldview, it's not inappropriate to begin the sermon inductively with them. Remember, we are part of the postmodern milieu too, and it affects our understanding of matters of faith more than we'd care to admit. The goal of the introduction is to show that the church needs hope too.

For this sermon it's important for you, the reader, to understand some context. It was preached in the mid-1990s, in the waning years of a controversy that had raged between conservative and moderate Southern Baptists. Since I was a faculty member at the Southern Baptists' flagship seminary, I was deeply affected by circumstances surrounding that conflict. I use this story and the final story of the sermon as testimonials to the power of calling and hope in our faith. Again, the use of narrative to appeal to the sensibilities of postmodern minds is intentional.

"On Eagle's Wings"
Isaiah 40:28–31; Luke 8:18–23

Often this famous passage from Isaiah rises to the top of my mind. It pops up at what might seem to be strange and inappropriate times. As I wait for a traffic light to change from red to green, or stroll the aisles at the grocery store or watch children frolicking on a playground, or listening to Mozart or the Maranatha Band, there it comes: "Those who wait for the LORD shall renew their strength."

The passage also comes at more expected times. A couple of years ago I was in Macon, Georgia, to preach a revival. Our services were scheduled from Sunday morning through Wednesday evening. On Saturday night we gathered in the sanctuary to pray. And Isaiah's words popped up between the tattered pages of a church's story.

It was a painful story—a story compelled by grief over the painful departure of a pastor; the lament of strong and ugly words spoken in haste; the fear of relationships lost; the despair of a people wondering if they would ever be able to be church again. I was there to preach in revival services, a revival that had been planned for well over a year. They gathered together for prayer, reluctantly, out of obligation, just going through the motions. With heads bowed and eyes closed, we gathered in the sanctuary to pray. For twenty minutes no one spoke. The sound of silence choked the room. Here we sat in a place of public worship, yet no one could speak. The pain of the immediate past muzzled their voices.

Then it began. Only a trickle at first. One soul, one quivering voice, "God, please forgive me." A second voice, through choked-back tears, entered the chorus: "Heavenly Father, help us." After some time a third, then a fourth—trembling voices, fearing their own sound, indicted by their own words, clinging to some faint hope, real hope, that maybe, just maybe, God had not forsaken them. Was God still listening? Could God still hear their prayers?

As I listened—sitting still in the pew, my head bowed—my thoughts raced. I had not been warned about the pain; no one had told me about the grief. How do I preach among such a painfully disrupted community?

The answer came as swiftly as an ocean wave pounds the sandy beach. Those words that wash over me when I least expect them: "Those who wait . . ." Isaiah said.

When it came time to consider my sermon for this morning, like a voice crying in the wilderness, I heard Isaiah's words again. What was the passage's motivation for returning? Was it a long-lost friend arriving to offer encouragement, or was it that person, that annoying person, who sits next to you on every airplane and has to talk to make their flight more pleasant? I wasn't sure. "Those who wait for the LORD shall renew their strength, they shall mount up with wings like eagles, they shall run and not be weary, they shall walk and not faint."

But why these words? Why now? Isaiah foresaw the eventual exile of Jerusalem. In the early sixth century B.C. an event as significant as the exodus of the Israelites from Egypt overtook Jerusalem. The people were stripped of their possessions, all they considered important, and were torn from their homeland and carried away in captivity to Babylon. Isaiah spoke to the situation of the exiles—those ripped from their homeland by hostile forces, those placed in a distant land with strange customs and foreign ways. These are words of hope for an oppressed people, a lonely, struggling people, clinging with bloodied fingers to faith elusive.

Was this the text I should use for today? No other idea captured my mind. No other text seemed more obvious. But why? But how? Because no other text seemed less appropriate. The best of the baby-boomer and baby-buster generations are represented here. The senior adults here are vibrant and spirited. Talented youth, vivacious children. There are no exiles here! In comparison to Isaiah's audience, this congregation resembles a Norman Rockwell portrait.

As I reflected on the text, I began to wonder, again, why Isaiah's words appeared so important to me. The autobiography began to unfold in my mind.

My sabbatical leave from the seminary was both the best of times and the worst of times. It offered me some distance from the strife tearing up that community. But not distance enough. Colleagues would phone, voicing dismay over the low morale of faculty and students. They asked me if I planned to return following my sabbatical—or was I going to be able "to get out," as one friend expressed it? *Get out,* I thought, *that's the language prisoners use. Get out?*

My mind raced; thoughts and questions flowed: If I stayed at the seminary, some friends would write me off. Some already had: "He sold out," they said. *Some friends,* I thought. I discovered that neither side in the denominational mess had a monopoly on intolerance!

Some faculty friends encouraged any of us who could leave to go before it was too late. Other faculty colleagues said we had to stay, now more than ever. I was supposed to be on sabbatical leave—a time of development from which I could return to the classroom renewed and refreshed.

Our trip to Denmark in July 1995 couldn't have come at a better time. It offered us distance—metaphorically and actually—from Louisville, the seminary, the Southern Baptist Convention, friends and antagonists alike. For the first few days there, Aunchalee and I never mentioned our future. We were with family who never heard of and would never care about what happened in Southern Baptistland. How refreshing! I tried to believe that the world and God's kingdom did not stand or fall on the fate of the SBC. While we were in Denmark, my hunch was made clear.

In the quietness of the trees behind our family's house, I prayed. And in the midst of that prayer my answer came. In 1988 when I had gone to the Southern Baptist Theological Seminary to teach, I went with an overwhelming sense that God had called me to that place. It was not some whimsical decision on my part or on God's part. Here appears no capricious God who enjoys watching people struggle with life.

My mind was made up. I would return to the classroom, to theological education, to students, and I would put the best I had into my teaching ministry. I had always said, "God called me here, and I will be here until God calls me to another ministry." The gospel demands no less. And to my cynical friends who wouldn't understand, who'd say I was in denial, who'd claim I'd sold out, my graceful response: "Get a life!"

I wasn't being naive. At that point I knew the future would not always be rosy. There was much about the seminary and the denomination that I find totally outside my realm of tolerance, beyond my comfort zone. It's there that I hope I can cling, with bloodied fingers if necessary, to Isaiah's words: "Those who wait for the LORD shall renew their strength, they shall mount up with wings like eagles, they shall run and not be weary, they shall walk and not faint."

"When there is no occasion to soar and no place to run, and all you can do is trudge along step by step, to hear of a Help that will enable you to 'walk and not faint' is good news indeed," wrote John Claypool, in *Tracks of a Fellow Struggler.*[6]

I've come to realize that Isaiah's words are not just for exiles. These words come to all pilgrims of faith who wonder at one time or another if God cares, if God is real, if God works, where God is, why I am being laid off, why the plant is closing. Isaiah's words say that God is not arbitrary.

Frank Tupper relates a telephone conversation he had with a former student.[7] "Dr. Tupper," the student said, "do you remember David? We sat together in your theology class."

Frank remembered David, "a hearty, vigorous man."

The student continued: "Did you know that David is ill? David is dying. He would like to hear from you. Would you call him?"

Answering with little hesitation, Frank said, "No, I don't think I can call him. I would not know anything that I could say to him." Frank Tupper was still experiencing pain over the death of his wife the previous September.

"I'm sorry. If I had known, I probably would not have called." The conversation ended awkwardly.

Two days later Frank decided to call David, then a pastor in Kentucky.

"Hello, David, this is Frank Tupper in Louisville."

"Hello, Dr. Tupper."

There was awkward talk, bridging the miles between them, between the death now at work in David and the death long worked over Frank. He asked David how he felt. They talked about David's medication, his therapies, how it made him feel.

After a long pause, David asked: "Dr. Tupper, is God arbitrary?"

Frank's mind raced with more questions than answers: "Is God arbitrary? Is God consistent? Am I dying because God simply refuses through medicine or miracle to heal me? Am I leaving my wife and baby son because God thinks they really do not need me? Am I sick to death because God has some judgment against me for some wrong long forgotten in the forgiveness of grace? Fact: Am I dying because God does not love me enough to make me well?"

"No, David," said Frank Tupper, "God is not arbitrary. God always does the most God can do."

David replied, almost in a whisper, "No . . . That's what I thought."

A few days later, Frank called David again. The conversation proved less intense. They talked about life and its many gifts. They talked about death and the hope of eternal life. David listened, occasionally questioning. But he had already asked and answered the crucial question, the God question.

Tupper writes: "Now the pain of saying 'Good-bye' occupied him much more than the contemplation of saying 'Hello.' He died a short time later, but he faced death believing: Life is arbitrary. God is not. Grace."

In Summary

This chapter addressed the question, Is it possible to preach hope in an era of skepticism? It addressed the possibilities for offering hope to people who have become cynical and skeptical about matters religious. This chapter showed how hope is at the heart of Christian faith and how faithful preaching of the gospel can bring promise to hope-starved people.

In the next chapter we continue our quest for effective apologetic preaching. How do we proclaim confidence in a time of doubt?

4

Proclaiming Confidence in a Time of Doubt

A CCORDING TO POSTMODERN THEORISTS, UNCERTAINTY REMAINS the only thing certain. Descartes's philosophical venture put everything in doubt so as to find something that could not be doubted. The postmodern climate provokes doubt not for the sake of philosophical inquiry but because of the inherent pessimism of the age. Perceptions distort experience. Experience can misinterpret facts. Reality is a mental construct. Absolutes are a myth of an earlier, naive generation. Such goes the wisdom of postmodernity.

As a faith grounded in human history, Christianity has always made its proclamation from the ground of confidence. Facts, evidence and testimonies became the core of the early church's proclamation. Faith emerged as a confluence of conviction and confidence. First John 1:1-3 reflect the certainty of early Christian proclamation:

> We declare to you what was from the beginning, what we have *heard*, what we have *seen with our eyes*, what we have *looked at* and *touched with our hands*, concerning the word of life—this life was revealed, and we have seen it and testify to it, and declare to you the eternal life that was with the Father

and was revealed to us—we declare to you what we have seen and heard so that you also may have fellowship with us; and truly our fellowship is with the Father and with his Son Jesus Christ.

Can Christianity's confidence scale the wall of postmodernity's doubt? The explanation for postmodernism's doubt dovetails from the reasons this age experiences its sense of skepticism. The previous chapter detailed those reasons. This chapter explores a theological defense for proclaiming confidence in a doubting time. If hope is the Christian response to skepticism, faith is the Christian response to doubt.

Doubt Versus Faith

As we begin considering this topic, we must be careful not to vilify doubt. Doubt in and of itself is not bad or evil. As a matter of fact, where religious systems are at stake, healthy doubt prevents blind allegiance, which can be destructive. Jim Jones and David Koresh demanded total and unequivocal allegiance; doubt would not be tolerated in their systems of thought. A degree of healthy doubt among their followers might have prevented the tragic loss of life in both situations. When someone—*anyone*—demands total, blind loyalty at any price and is intolerant of doubt, destruction looms on the horizon.

We've all struggled with doubt at one time or another. In dark nights of the soul we may doubt the very existence of God. In the face of the death of a loved one, we might cry out, "God, if you are all-knowing and all-powerful, why didn't you do something?" The age-old inquiry into why and how a loving God allows bad things to happen to good people appears to call religious faith into serious question. During World War II, victims of the Holocaust put God on trial and found him guilty for neglecting millions of Jews who died at the hands of Nazis. Even Jesus' cry from the cross, "My God, my God, why have you forsaken me?" could be described as a cry of doubt.

But in these cries, permeated as they are by doubt, the reality of God and God's presence whispers. For even when we doubt God, the presence of

God breaks through. The questioning of God shows faith in God rather than doubt of God's existence. Ultimately, faith overcomes doubt. A questioning doubt often leads to greater faith. We are inclined to avoid the pilgrimage of walking through doubt to faith, yet it may be the most beneficial journey of all. So doubt, in and of itself, may not be bad.

But the current cultural doubt—tied closely to the skepticism of our age—almost becomes doubt for doubt's sake, a kind of end in and of itself. Here is not doubt in the pursuit of further understanding but doubt aiming to debunk any standard or traditional system of thought—including religious systems—as archaic and meaningless. Here doubt is being used as an antidote for perceived intolerance within religious systems. Doubt is the presenting face of a pseudo-intellectualism that presumes only new ways of thought could have any meaningful consequences for postmodern culture. Postmodern theorists view faith systems as mere products of an earlier age of myth and superstition. Hence they doubt religion's veracity and ability to provide meaning in a culture where understanding can be grasped without reliance on antiquated concepts of religious belief.

Even Descartes's doubting led to a positive understanding; in his doubting it came to him: "I think, therefore I am." The doubt of the postmodern era does not appear to have such noble goals.

Faith, on the other hand—Christian faith in particular—could be defined along the lines of thought of Thomas Aquinas, as doubt in search of understanding. In Aquinas's system the starting point for human knowledge was reason. But when we look at life honestly, it becomes obvious that reason can carry one's understanding of human experience only so far. Our human experience is wrapped in enough mystery that reason often leaves us lacking understanding of our times and circumstances.

We do not reason why a sunset is beautiful; the beauty is mysteriously self-evident. We do not reason why a child smiles at the sight of her mother; love's mystery requires no explanation. At some point, Aquinas said, faith overlaps reason and enables us to further understand our experiences and situations. But at still a further point, reason falls totally by the wayside, completely incapable of providing any explanation for what is taking place around us. From that moment forward, Aquinas presumed, faith must be fully operative. Faith takes over when reason fails.

We might try to apply the same perspective within our current discussion of faith and doubt. Faith takes over from doubt when doubt no longer provides the meaningful explanation for our experiences, circumstances or situations.

My presumption is that to live always succumbing to doubt's overtures about life would be to live in a very depressed state. That's why for Descartes, the discovery that doubt led to a new understanding of who he was became a moment of liberation. Authentic faith offers such liberation to our doubting age.

What about the age's faith in science and doubt of religion? The popular 1997 science-fiction film *Contact* was based on a 1985 Carl Sagan novel. Jodie Foster plays a radio astronomer, Ellie Arroway, who has been fascinated with science since she was a child experimenting with her father's shortwave radio. As a radio astronomer, Ellie searches for signs of extraterrestrial intelligence. One night while scanning radio frequencies from distant planets, she discovers a strong signal from the distant star Vega. The radio signal obviously originates from an intelligent source, and Ellie's life is transformed forever.

Due to the nature of the discovery, the government gets involved. Further investigation of the radio signal reveals that its subfrequencies contain the blueprints for constructing a transport capable of sending a traveler to another world.

In an attempt to retain control of the discovery, Ellie turns to a former acquaintance and now presidential spiritual adviser, Palmer Joss. Joss supports her but questions her belief in science over religion. While we are never told, Ellie's doubts about religion appear to originate in the death of both her parents when she was a child. Ellie doesn't believe in God, or in any religion, because she needs concrete facts to support any belief, and she can't find them. She's searching for answers that she believes are scientific, yet she finds herself questioning her "faith" in science and learns that religion might not be such a hard thing to accept after all. Palmer questions whether science can fill the void in people's lives and fulfill their search for meaning.

An underlying theme of the film is a tug-and-pull relationship between science and religion. Can religion and science coexist? Such is the question postmodernists pose. It is an unnecessary dichotomy when religion and science are each understood in their appropriate realm of operation. Science does a wonderful job of explaining the *whys* and *hows* of physical phenomena, but when it comes to matters of faith, science flounders. Faith cannot adequately explain how atoms function to create molecules and how molecules become the building blocks for all matter. However, faith does answer the question about how a family faces the death of a loved one with hope. When science and faith work within their proper spheres, they complement rather than contradict each other.

Christianity 101

How does one begin to define the basic tenets of the Christian faith? Is there a source we can use to find what makes Christianity unique from other religions? While my own denomination is confessional rather than creedal, the creeds of the early church certainly provide a framework for viewing the landscape of the crucial elements of Christianity. C. E. B. Cranfield, in *The Apostles' Creed: A Faith to Live By,* describes the creed as "a compact and felicitous summary of New Testament teaching."[1] The text of the Apostles' Creed that appears below is a modern version of the original and points out some basic tenets of Christian faith:

> I believe in God, the Father almighty,
> creator of heaven and earth.
> I believe in Jesus Christ, his only Son, our Lord.
> He was conceived by the power of the Holy Spirit
> and born of the Virgin Mary.
> He suffered under Pontius Pilate,
> was crucified, died, and was buried.

He descended to the dead.
On the third day he rose again.
He ascended into heaven
and is seated at the right hand of the Father.
He will come again to judge the living and the dead.
I believe in the Holy Sprit,
the holy catholic church,
the communion of saints,
the forgiveness of sins,
the resurrection of the body,
and the life everlasting.[2]

The creed comprises some basic tenets of the faith that are universally understood as part of Christian teaching. What do we hold to be certain?

The creed portrays a triune deity consisting of God as Father, Son and Holy Spirit. Though the Bible does not contain the word *trinity*, biblical revelation shows that the God of the Bible is one God who manifests himself in three persons: Father, Son and Holy Spirit. The triune nature of God is critical to Christian faith.

God the Father is the very Creator of heaven and earth. Here we see that God is not a manifestation of nature, subsumed under the powers of natural order. God represents the creative power behind the universe and all that exists. God also "reigns with providential care" over the universe and all that he created there.[3] In Scripture, God is revealed as all-powerful, all-loving and all-wise.

The creed speaks of Jesus Christ as the eternal Son of God. Here the mystery of incarnation crashes headlong into the sensibilities of postmodern thought. In Jesus Christ the fullness of deity and humanity are manifested. Conceived by the Holy Spirit, he is fully God; born of the Virgin Mary, he is fully human. Suffering under Pontius Pilate, being crucified, dying and being buried, he is fully human. Rising from the dead and ascending into heaven, sitting at the Father's side, he is fully divine. The weaving of Christ's humanity and divinity is a hinge pin of Christian faith.

A story is told about a Kansas family that lived through a tornado that nearly destroyed their home. From that point on the little daughter became terribly frightened every time the sky darkened and storm winds began to blow. She thought another tornado was on its way.

One evening a great thunderstorm developed. The torrent of rain, the loud thunder, the cracking of lightning frightened the girl. When her bedtime came, she was afraid to go upstairs to her bed. Her parents took her and tucked her in. However, from the living room they could hear her crying, so the father went up to see if he could calm her fears.

"There's no reason to cry. It's only a thunderstorm. It'll soon be over. Now there's no reason for you to be scared or afraid."

To this the little girl responded, "Yeah, Daddy, that's easy for you to say. You don't know what it's like to be little!"

The incarnation of Jesus Christ reminds us that God knows what it's like to be human. And because he knows, he understands us, even better than we understand ourselves. The incarnation makes no sense rationally, but in faith it remains utterly sensible.

The creed portrays the Holy Spirit as the active person of God in the world—from empowering creation, to the conceiving of Christ, to the enabling of the church. The Holy Spirit enables Christian unity and communion. The Holy Spirit "convicts of sin, of righteousness,"[4] and effects regeneration and the forgiveness of sins.

Further elements of Christian faith are only implied in the creed but are certainly supported by it. Christian faith transcends a system of belief. Trust in Jesus Christ becomes a living faith as we live out the very commandments Jesus urged upon his followers. What Christians call the Great Commission becomes the banner under which Christ's followers live out their faith in the world: "Go therefore and make disciples of all nations, baptizing them in the name of the Father and of the Son and of the Holy Spirit, and teaching them to obey everything that I have commanded you. And remember, I am with you always, to the end of the age" (Mt 28:19–20).

What did Jesus expect from his followers? His inaugural sermon in

Luke's Gospel (4:16–21) and the Sermon on the Mount certainly offer ample evidence: Christ's followers will make sure the poor are not forgotten. Oppressed people will be liberated. Broken families will be reconciled. Lustful behavior will be transformed. Generosity will be a way of life. Live by what you speak; speak the way you live. Random acts of kindness will be performed because it's the right thing to do, not in quest of some selfish gain. Faith will be practiced for its own sake, not so others will think better of us. Enemies will be prayed for and loved. Life will begin to reflect or foreshadow God's kingdom, where tears and pain do not exist and where all people are equal in God's eyes.

Christian faith, rooted in the incarnation of Jesus Christ, is faith lived out in the trenches of real-life circumstances and situations. It takes into account the ordinary struggles of existence and the big questions of life: Why am I here? Can I make a difference? Is there meaning in my life? The Christian faith, in its profession and practice, answers loudly, Yes!

How can we be certain? Because Christians offer testimony to the transformation they have experienced as followers of—not merely believers in—Jesus Christ. The practical side of faith that moves it from the realm of doubt to the spaces of confidence. The living, breathing communities of forgiveness, love and reconciliation bear witness to the transforming goodness of a God who loves all people.

The question might be asked, What are the bases for our affirmations of Christian faith? Obviously the witness and testimonies of the early Christians, many of which are described in the Gospels themselves. From eyewitness accounts, the stories of a life became the basis for a faith. Here is where the subjective and objective meet in faith. Hence we are not calling for blind allegiance or loyalty. We are basing faith on the accounts of witnesses. From their understanding, faith carries us forward when doubt and reason fail. The same certainty is claimed and proclaimed by believers today. The greatest apologetic for the doubt of the age is the confidence that not only surrounds Christians' belief but motivates our faith. James was right: "So faith by itself, if it has no works, is dead" (Jas 2:17). Proclaiming confidence is possible because Christians live and move and have their being living out the reality of their faith.

Proclaiming Confidence

As mentioned in chapter one, earlier apologetics were based on Western logic systems, strongly influenced by Aristotle. The syllogistic method was the apologetic tool of choice. Faith statements were developed logically and rationally, appealing to reason and the intellect of the hearer. Apologists presumed that the reason people did not respond to the gospel was that they were ignorant concerning its content. The goal of these early apologists was to enlighten people's minds and remove their ignorance. They presumed that people will act on the truth once they know it. Hence the apologetic method was to merely lay out the truth in a logical and straightforward way. The apologetic method was rational and deductive.

An Aristotelian syllogism would go like this:

Major premise: All people are mortal.
Minor premise: Socrates was a person.
Conclusion: Therefore Socrates was mortal.

The conclusion is drawn from a logical progression, based on the major and minor premises. A more contemporary example would be as follows:

Major premise: All green apples are sour.
Minor premise: This is a green apple.
Conclusion: Therefore this green apple is sour.

This kind of logic moves from a general principle to a specific situation. At the heart of this logical apologetic approach lies *an unquestioned acceptance of the proposition that constitutes the major premise.*

What happens, though, if the major premise is not accepted? In deductive logic, if the major premise appears unacceptable, there's no place for the logic to move.

Based on my own preaching experience more than on a widespread study, I suggest that postmodern people will have to be convinced differently. They do not assume the major premises of Christian faith. The logical system described above stands or falls on the acceptance of the major premise. When that adherence is not present, the system of logic is useless.

A postmodern apologetic must tap into the culture's desire for story and meaning based on narrative assumptions. Apologetic preaching must build on the Christian story and weave it into the fabric of the culture's story. Our preaching can weave the hope apparent in the nativity into the need for hope in the lives of our postmodern neighbors. We can show how the sacrifice of Christ touches the sensitivities of people who typically don't understand the concept of sacrifice in any realm of their lives. Our sermons can build on the culture's desire for relationships and show how the gospel story breaks down all barriers between people. By intentionally looking for places of connection between the gospel and the postmodern world—being careful not to demonize postmodernism—we will move our listeners by identifying with their life experiences.

Induction derives general principles from particular instances. Inductive logic moves from particular experience to forming a general principle. Most of the life-experience wisdom we have we've learned inductively. You can tell a child, until your face turns blue, that they shouldn't come near a hot oven or they will get burned. Most kids learn the truth of that proposition only when they touch a hot oven. What they failed to learn deductively they discover inductively.

Here is an example of inductive logic. Suppose you've never eaten a green apple and no one has told you what to expect when you eat green apples. You bite into one and discover that it tastes sour. Can you draw a conclusion about all green apples based on your experience with one? Not yet. But after you've eaten a half-dozen or so green apples, though no one has said anything to you about them, you draw the conclusion that green apples are sour. That is the general principle you have discovered inductively through experience. The conclusion you've drawn is "Green apples are sour." You came to this conclusion through an informal process of discovery.

Christian faith does not need to be argued as much as it needs to be shared. Will Willimon said to me once that his biggest challenge in preaching today is just getting the story straight. In previous generations a preacher's listeners knew the story. If you didn't get it right, they'd know it and they'd call your hand on it. Today people don't know the story and the stories of our faith. While preaching to earlier generations, a preacher could make allusions to David's sin, Abraham's faith or Peter's denial and see nods of understanding. Today if you mentioned David's sin without a further explanation, many of your hearers would have virtually no idea what you were talking about. And an unchurched person who wandered in off the street might think that if you are speaking about David's sin this week, you might be talking about his sin next week. That person just might not return!

Apologetic preaching that is powerful to postmodern ears must not rely totally on the deductive homiletic methods outlined above; instead we must find communication approaches that will be effective vehicles for carrying the scandalous message of the gospel. More inductive models, along with the rich use of biblical narrative, will help postmodern listeners hear the difficult message that God loves them and has acted on their behalf in Jesus Christ. Gaining such a hearing is the ultimate goal of apologetic preaching.

Proclaiming Confidence in Faith

Our proclamation of confidence is rooted in faith. And faith offers real meaning, hope and, yes, even confidence in a time of doubt. Postmodern people, while clinging to doubt, long for some way of making meaning in their lives. Authentic Christian faith—living, breathing the heartbeat of Jesus Christ—has the power not merely to inform but to transform even the staunchest doubter.

The sermon below illustrates preaching confidence in faith. I chose the Jonah story because it is a passage rife with places for doubt from a postmodern perspective. The debate mentioned in the sermon's introduction illustrates the issues that cause people to doubt the story's veracity. Once the story is doubted, we have a tendency to doubt God, who is the real mover in the story.

The sermon deals with the possibility of faith when the basis for faith seems irrational. The sermon rhetorically asks, "Is Christian faith hinged on finding that fish?" The sermon points out that "only children of the Enlightenment would ask such questions." By confronting such modern notions, the sermon aims to gain a hearing among postmodern listeners who reject the tenets of ultra-rationalism.

The sermon addresses postmodern doubt by showing that faith is not contingent upon scientifically verifiable truth. Factual knowledge is not the only way for communicating faith. Our movement from confidence to faith is based on the life of Jesus Christ. As the sermon states: "Having a kingdom view of life, seeing things from an eternal perspective, we see people through Jesus' eyes." The goal of the sermon is to move people from their doubt (created by their inability to believe the story of the fish) to faith, by unapologetically proclaiming the love of God as the source of our faith. The message of the sermon is Jesus and his power to change lives and prepare people for eternity. He is both the subject and the object of our faith. We proclaim that message in confidence, as the sermon attempts to illustrate.

"Who Knows? God May Change His Mind"

Jonah 3:1-10

When we were in South Florida in the late 1970s, several pastors were involved in a rather interesting debate. *Feud* would be a better word for it. The feud focused on questions related to the fish that swallowed Jonah: What kind of fish was it? Was it a sea monster? How big was the fish? Did the fish have teeth? Did eating Jonah give the fish indigestion? Was there such a fish that could swallow a man whole and three days later spit him out?

The point of the discussions—which, if my memory serves me correctly, went on for an awfully long time, probably about a year—was to be able to empirically, rationally and unequivocally identify the kind of fish that swallowed Jonah, thereby proving, beyond the shadow of a doubt, that the biblical account was true. It seemed that the Christian faith hinged on finding that fish.

Of course, only children of the Enlightenment would ask such questions. The pastors, thinking they were doing theology, were merely parroting seventeenth-century rationalism. They presumed that only the scientifically verifiable is true. And if they couldn't deduce it through human thought processes—rationalism—it must not be true. They left no place for faith, or wonder, or even the miraculous. When they preached they talked about God, about the Bible, about life. They acted as if they were viewing God and the Bible like specimens under a microscope. They presumed that factual information was the only way of communicating religious truth. So their sermons were marked by unending attempts to locate Noah's ark or to describe the fish big enough to swallow Jonah. They attempted rationally to prove the truthfulness of the biblical accounts.

A strange venture, indeed, by those who claimed total reliance on the Bible. And actually their sermons raised doubts about the Bible's accuracy, because all its claims had to be verified within common human experience. An odd mix for pastors who could cite Hebrews 11:1 from memory: "Now faith is the assurance of things hoped for, the conviction of things not seen." Unfortunately, to them *faith* unwittingly became a synonym for *rationalism.* Those pastors thought they were children of Abraham. They were really children of Descartes.

A close reading of the text shows that the fish is just a bit player in the drama, little more than an extra on the set. And Jonah's up to his neck in the plot—figuratively and literally. The main character is—God!

In chapter 3 God comes to the prophet Jonah again and says: "Get up, go to Nineveh, that great city, and proclaim to it the message that I tell you." That's essentially the same thing God said to Jonah before his little jaunt in the belly of the fish. It just goes to show you that the old adage is true: "When it comes to God, you can run, but you can't hide!" Though Jonah heads for Nineveh this time, he's no happier than he was before his little fishcapade.

Nineveh was a very large city. But the biblical writer is less concerned with the size of the city than with the city's importance as an Assyrian capital. The narrator's point is that Nineveh was a "three-day visit city," a major diplomatic center of the ancient world. Official visitors followed a formal protocol. It took three days to make an official visit. Because of Nineveh's importance and size, Jonah would have to preach there for at least three days, to be sure that God's message had been heard by all the people.

On the first day, Jonah enters the city and proclaims: "In just forty days, Nineveh is going to be overthrown!" Now, in some other Old Testament prophets we can detect a tone of sadness in their voice when they bring such a message. Jonah sounds like a kid on the playground yelling at some bullies: "You're gonna get yours!" But Jonah is unprepared for the response his preaching elicits.

Do you get the irony? Jonah hates the Ninevites. He doesn't want to preach to them. He figures he's in for three days' worth of screaming at them to get them to repent, which he is sure they would never do. *People like them don't deserve to hear God*, he thinks. Yet the Ninevites beat him to the punch. They repent before he can really get started. Jonah is just warming up and they are already believing God, in droves. Like the Hebrew women who gave birth before the midwives could arrive, the Ninevites respond to God's message almost before Jonah starts his sermon!

As soon as the people heard what Jonah had to say, they stopped eating and began changing into sackcloth, the mourning garb of the ancient Near East. Everyone took part, from the nobility to the poor. The response of faith and repentance was citywide in scope.

What Jonah was afraid might happen was happening! But it baffled his expectations. Even the king covered himself in sackcloth and sat in ashes. Listen again to the king's decree:

> No human being or animal, no herd or flock, shall taste anything. They shall not feed, nor shall they drink water. Human beings and animals shall be covered with sackcloth, and they shall cry mightily to God. All shall turn from their evil ways and from the violence that is in their hands. Who knows? God may relent and change his mind; he may turn from his fierce anger, so that we do not perish.

Jonah's message had certainly been well received. The king and the people repented. When God saw what they did, how they turned from their evil ways, God changed his mind about the calamity that he had said he would bring upon them.

The king's decree and the people's repentance capture what Jonah resentfully understood all along: God can forgive anybody, even a city known for its wildness, which had oppressed Jonah's own people. God was everything Jonah feared and the sinful city hoped. As a result of the genuine repentance of the people, God relented, simply and fully, of his original plan to punish them. Jonah's mission had had a wonderful effect!

But Jonah was angry: "Lord, isn't this what I said would happen? That's why I fled to Tarshish in the first place. I just knew you were a gracious God and merciful, slow to get mad, and full of love, and always ready to change your mind about punishing. I'd rather die than see what I just saw!"

Then Jonah left the city and sat down, waiting to see what would happen. God made a bush grow, and it provided shade for Jonah from the scorching heat. Jonah was quite happy about the bush. But then God sent a worm to destroy the bush, and it withered. The next day was terribly hot, so hot that Jonah wished he were dead.

But God said to Jonah: "Is it right for you to be angry about the bush?"

"Yes, angry enough to die," Jonah argued.

Then God said, "You are concerned about the bush. You didn't plant it; you didn't nurture it to grow. It grew one day and was gone the next. And shouldn't I be concerned about Nineveh, in which there are more that a hundred twenty thousand persons who do not know their right hand from their left, and also many animals?"

Jonah the nationalist wants God to bless Israel and harm all its enemies. God did indeed love more than just Israel. He loved—to Jonah's horror—the Assyrians.

Jonah is haunted by those two questions: "Who knows?" asked the king, "God might change his mind." And God's question: "Shouldn't I be concerned about the lives of the people of Nineveh?"

The book of Jonah shows that God is a merciful and forgiving God, longing for people to repent and love him, longing to change doubt into faith, longing to make life—real life—possible. Our lives are ours on trust from God. All of human life is sacred, from its mysterious origin to its mysterious end.

A popular evangelical author was answering questions about a new book during a radio call-in talk show. The callers "wanted to talk about how terrible television is, how awful the movies are, about prayer in public schools, about the homosexual agenda, about abortion, about pornography and child abuse, about sex education, and about politics. The disturbing thing is that most of the callers thought they were talking about Jesus!"[5]

Having a kingdom view of life, seeing things from an eternal perspective, we see people through Jesus' eyes. We will bypass the cruel slogans and the stereotypical buzz words and the "bumper sticker" theology, and become more deeply and more intimately involved. When we view the sanctity of life through Jesus' eyes, it will cause us to penetrate every human activity with the salt of the gospel. The gospel will cause us to change our timing, strategies, approaches, procedures and goals. We will never use methods to save lives on earth that will drive people away from the Savior and eternal life. It might be easier to protest, to be arrested and even to spend time in jail than it is to commit ourselves to the gospel demand to love people, to serve them and to win them for Jesus Christ. God forbid that what we do politically, thinking we are being righteous, might actually drive people from Jesus rather than drawing people to him.

People in our community should know the gospel message: Jesus and his power to change lives and prepare people for eternity with him.

In Summary

This chapter addressed the question, Is it possible to preach confidence in a time of doubt? For a variety of reasons, the postmodern worldview approaches organized religion from a stance of doubt. While spirituality is readily embraced, issues of organized faith are viewed doubtfully. This chapter addressed the possibilities for offering confidence to a doubting people.

In the next chapter we turn our attention to another challenge for us as preachers: proclaiming truth in a climate of relativism.

5

Proclaiming Truth in a Climate of Relativism

THE POSTMODERN WORLD EXISTS ON MULTIPLE UNDERSTANDINGS of reality, highly skeptical of any objective view of truth. In fact, the notion of absolute truth is seen as an oxymoron in the pluralized epoch of postmodernism. Postmodernists harbor no concept of absolute, universal or objective truth. Matters of truth are relative. It all depends on whom you ask, suggests the postmodernist. Just as beauty is in the eye of the be-holder, truth is in the mind of the believer. Truth, rather than being an external reality, becomes merely a belief in the mind of its holder. In matters of religion, philosophy or morals, one system's viewpoint offers as much validity as another, one person's opinion is as sound as another's. To postmodern minds, truth is an internalized construct rather than an external reality.

In this strange new world, people expect a variety of truth options. If the cross of Christianity is too gruesome, they can choose the serenity of the Buddha. If Buddhism is too introspective, they can opt for the communal aspirations of the New Age. One religious choice is expected to contain as much truth as another. "It doesn't really matter what you believe, as long as you believe something" is the mantra of many postmodern seekers. In actual practice postmodern thinking is eclectic, picking and choosing among the plethora of thought available. It's also extremely utilitarian, choosing what works in the moment and discarding it when its useful life passes.

As I think about church life at the dawn of a new millennium, it's obvious that church people have not escaped the effects of relativism. That should not surprise us, because the church today cannot escape the influence of postmodernism. Nor should it. We must be careful not to demonize postmodernism and exalt modernism. Each has its strengths and weaknesses. Each has influence on the people in the pews. Our goal as preachers is to learn how to effectively proclaim the gospel in the immediate context in which we find ourselves. Our current context is permeated by the postmodern worldview.

When it comes to mystery, the postmodern world appears pliable. Hope can sometimes coax an expression of longing from even the most pessimistic skeptic. Exceptionally conditioned doubters nod to a glimmer of certainty now and again. In the postmodern world, however, *truth* is tantamount to a four-letter word. Relativism has become a religion unto itself. Any attempt to claim a sole view of truth seems hidebound, illiberal and sectarian.

This chapter argues that irony floats in the air of our discussion. The pluralism of the age has actually set a place at the table for Christianity. Now Christian apologetics has the opportunity, as a viable conversation partner, to present its case.

During the Christian era, Christian apologists assumed *their* place at the table because it was their table, set upon their understandings of reality. They were not always gracious allowing others to join them at the table. However, in a post-Christian time, Judeo-Christian assumptions no longer hold sway. They were so rejected by holders of other religious and philosophical positions that, in effect, these others got up from the table and left the room. Christian apologists didn't lose their place at the table; they were left with a table that no one else seemed to care about.

But now the pluralistic players of the age—under the standard of tolerance and openness—have invited Christians to join them at their table. It is a large table, with place settings of every ilk and persuasion. Nevertheless, at least Christians have an opportunity to explain their view of truth to waiting, though admittedly skeptical, listeners. This chapter offers a theological rationale for preaching truth in such a climate of relativism.

Dominance of the Subjective, Loss of the Objective

The story is told of three baseball umpires discussing how they call pitches. The premodern umpire says, "I call 'em as they are!"

The modern umpire shakes his head and replies, "I call 'em as I see 'em."

With a smile of supreme confidence, the postmodern umpire retorts, "They ain't nothin' till I call 'em!"

Postmodernists normalize the subjective experience of individuals. The normalization of *my* experience as the experience for me dawned as a byproduct of late modernism. Some sociologists loosely term the 1970s the "me generation" and the 1980s the "my generation." But these two decades were constructs of the deinstitutionalization—or, better expressed, the anti-institutionalization—that came as part of the social movement among young people during the 1960s. The hippie movement made nonconformity popular. *Hippie* was a slang term used for persons who rejected standard societal customs, attitudes and lifestyles. "Do your own thing" became the hippie culture's approach to life. The generation's gurus questioned the values, mores, social norms and institutional loyalties of their parents. Anyone over thirty was suspect. *Thirtysomething* would be a pejorative moniker.

If you were over thirty, you probably had too much loyalty to the status quo, which was viewed by the younger generation as oppressive and inhibiting. Breaking out of one's inhibitions became a major life goal for the hippie—thus the proliferation of hallucinogenic drugs, primarily lysergic acid diethylamide (LSD). Such hallucinogens supposedly heightened awareness and provided the user with a view of reality as reality is meant to be experienced. Earlier generations used alcohol as the drug of choice to "drown their sorrows." Hippies rose above their "sorrows" with mind-altering, mind-enhancing drugs that created new realms of consciousness, or so they imagined. Those unwilling to journey down this road of heightened awareness were written off as narrow-minded and boorish. With mind-altering drugs, true believers were liberating themselves of the trappings of modern life that dominated society as they saw it.

While earlier generations of American teenagers and young adults had similarly tended to express disdain for their parents' ways of doing things, the generation moving from the 1960s into the 1970s threw everything up for grabs. From the God-is-dead movement to free love to communal living, theirs was a world they would name and then claim. The seeds for relativism were well planted.

An Excursus

I graduated from high school in 1968. Prior to graduation, I played drums in a rock 'n' roll band. Like many teenage males of my era, I dreamed that our band would become America's answer to the Beatles, who had invaded our territory earlier in the decade. Following graduation from high school—a feat that at the time bordered on the miraculous for me—I enlisted for four years in the Air Force. While many friends were making their way to a New England rock concert known as Woodstock, I was stationed in Thailand, serving a fighter squadron supporting the bombing of North Vietnam.

Like many of my peers, I had a hippie's heart, but my practice was more conventional than I cared to admit. I disliked the U.S. government. Why? I wasn't quite sure. It was the thing to do. Hey, wait a minute, I thought we were nonconformists!

Institutions were inherently suspect—the government, institutions of higher learning, religious institutions, especially the latter. The reason religious institutions attracted so much of our ire had to do with their seeming willingness to stay locked into a distant time and space. For us at that time, religion was anything but relevant. It didn't even attempt to be. Religious leaders had a patriarchal, condescending attitude: they knew best what people needed. What they desired was compliance with their rules and regulations; such conformity would ensure a happy life. Those kinds of institutions represented the epitome of all we hoped to shed—hierarchical power structures, conformism, legalism. So, like many of that generation, I gave up going to church. (Why? Probably just to aggravate my parents.)

Yet here's the irony. While disliking the government, I was serving in the military. While mistrusting institutions, I am now a part of the religious establishment. (That is still hard to admit in writing!) As a generation, we now reap the whirlwind of the changes we cried for, worked for. In the words of the great theologian Pogo, "We have met the enemy, and they is us."

Much of who we are and how we approach life, then, is absolutely autobiographical. And we church leaders cannot demonize postmodernism; we helped create it.

Dominance of the Subjective, Loss of the Objective (Continued)

With the roots of relativism becoming well established during the 1970s and 1980s, it's no wonder that a popular phrase in the 1990s was "Opinions are like belly buttons: everybody has one." The concept of the dominant subjective, while seemingly esoteric at first glance, is expressed simply and directly in the song made popular by crooner Frank Sinatra. The title: "My Way." The point of the song: no matter whether it was right or wrong, at least I did it my way. Another example can be found in the jingle of a famous fast-food restaurant. When you order food—remember how the jingle went?—you can "have it your way!"

Up to that time, when you ate fast food you had it their way. Theirs was a fast-food assembly line with a one-size-fits all menu. They put mustard and ketchup on all the hamburgers. Every burger got onions and pickles. If you didn't like what came on your hamburger, you picked it off yourself. If you didn't like the menu, you didn't eat there. That was that. I remember hearing my mother tell our daughter, on a trip to one of these burger places,

"If you don't like the pickles just take them off."

But with the dominance of the subjective, you design and create your own burger. The assembly line now conforms to your wishes. Why? Because if it doesn't, you'll go down the street to the fast-food restaurant that will. Competition between burger places exemplifies and encourages the subjectivist's worldview. If people can have their burgers just exactly the way they want them, then why can't their religion fit their norms of tolerance, believability and suitable framework?

At a conference on church growth I was in a group of several pastors discussing the newest church-growth strategies. One pastor of a fairly successful seeker-based congregation explained, "We never mention the crucifixion of Christ. It's too gruesome for a lot of our folk. If we talked about that, many would stop coming. So we focus on the resurrection instead. The resurrection of Jesus is a positive, hopeful message."

The rest of us weren't sure we heard him correctly. I couldn't keep my mouth shut. I asked, "Well don't they ever wonder how he died?"

He said, "To tell you the truth, no one ever asks!"

Call me old-fashioned, but when we allow the subjectivism of our hearers to undermine the objective realities of Christian faith, haven't we violated the integrity of the gospel? We'd be better off staying quiet and letting the rocks preach than to offer a version of Christianity so diluted that it becomes unrecognizable. The crucifixion is an objective reality that must be proclaimed with as much passion as the resurrection. If not, then Paul's words become nonsense: "But we proclaim Christ crucified, a stumbling block to Jews and foolishness to Gentiles, but to those who are the called, both Jews and Greeks, Christ the power of God and the wisdom of God" (1 Cor 1:23–24). Of course it may offend people's sensibilities. Sometimes truth does that.

Can We Have It Both Ways?

If the Christian truth option cannot be objectified—which of course I think it can—then the same lack of objectification holds for all other systems of thought. One cannot have it both ways. You cannot presume relativism when it's convenient and then make exclusive claims for your own truth option. If stealing another's possessions is wrong, it is always wrong. It cannot be right when I steal your jacket but wrong when you steal mine. Either all truth is relative or no truth is relative. I argue for the latter. Truth is never relative; truth is truth.

Perhaps the issues get stickier in a pluralistic culture where various religious systems make truth claims. Here the issue becomes not the lack of truth but juxtaposed truth claims. If Christianity holds the keys to truth, and Islam likewise claims a hold on truth, how can the real truth be determined?

Some assumptions need to be established: A claim to truth does not determine truthfulness. All truth comes from God. I believe that Jesus Christ is God's full and true revelation of himself to humankind. Where there is truth, no matter where it is found, it must be truth. Truth will not contradict itself. The validity of a truth claim is not determined by its adherents; otherwise truth would still be relative and somewhat subjective. While truth may be validated subjectively, truth is determined objectively, outside itself. Hence the final arbiter of what is true and what is not will be God.

The Parable of the Watch and the Watchmaker

The story of the watchmaker has often been used as a parable to make sense out of questions of objective realities. My rendition is a hybrid of the several versions available. A man is walking across the desert and stumbles across a pocket watch, its chain still attached. He snaps the watch open and turns the stem several times, and the small sweep hand begins to rotate. He puts the watch to his ear and hears it ticking. With a little finagling, he pops the back plate of the watch open to expose its mechanism. There, before his eyes, he sees rotating cogs and springs, gently turning to and fro, nudging the watch's hands forward. He thinks how amazing it is that someone could not only design such a timepiece but get all its working parts to fit so precisely into a confined space. He has never seen a watch before. But he assumes that such a fascinating instrument, with such remarkable complexity, has been created by someone. The watch demands a watchmaker.

For him to reach this conclusion is perfectly rational. It would be irrational for the wanderer to assume that the watch he finds springs simply from his own subjective experience. In fact, his life experience suggests the opposite: complex designs demand a designer. While exceptions to the rule might exist, that presupposition remains generally true. "This watch was made by a watchmaker" is a true statement that can be validated.

The example of the watchmaker points to the bigger reality: most of what we see and experience in life demands a Creator. The vastness of the universe, the miracle of human anatomy, the intricacies of the earth's ecosystem, the systemic nature of all that can be seen demand a Designer.

Postmoderns desire authentic explanations of the world. Careful observation of the earth around us yields the possibility of a Creator. Though postmodern thinkers might posit other possible scenarios for how the world and universe came into being, the Christian view of God as the Creator can be one option for them to consider. The pluralism of the age allows for that possibility, reminding us that postmodernism offers us opportunities for discussion and dialogue that modernism did not afford. The Christian apologist must find ways within a particular conversation or preaching moment to offer God as Creator as a very real possibility. One approach would be to preach the creation narratives not as science but as theological discourse to describe the origins of the universe. I have found that showing postmodern hearers that the biblical account is a theological description of historical reality, rather than a scientific treatise, taps into their understanding and desire for authenticity.

Jesus Our Model

When preaching truth and making exclusive claims for the veracity of Jesus Christ over other truth options or among those who claim that truth is relative, we do well to remember Peter's words: "Always be ready to make your defense to anyone who demands from you an accounting for the hope that is in you; yet do it with gentleness and reverence" (1 Pet 3:15–16). The operative words for our immediate discussion are *gentleness* and *reverence*.

I have been around evangelists and apologists who were always ready to give an account for the hope they had, but they wielded that accounting like a weapon. We sometimes joke about evangelists beating people over the head with the Bible to win their allegiance. While I don't think such an approach ever worked, it will most surely fail in this age. While the gospel itself may be an intrusive word, there is no need for those of us who preach to be personally offensive. Gentleness and reverence exemplify the stance we should take when we preach. The gospel demands no less, and Jesus himself will demand no more.

Jesus' words in John 14:6 focus our attention on this issue: "I am the way, and the truth, and the life." Since Jesus is the truth, we who proclaim his gospel could learn some homiletic methods from him.

First, Jesus never got in an argument with those who disagreed with him. He often responded to them with questions. He often told a pointed story. But he never lashed out in anger or ridicule. He spoke with *gentleness* and *reverence*. To argue and debate angrily over the truth of the gospel is to violate the good news we're attempting to share. Our methods should reflect the grace and glory of the Lord we proclaim.

Second, Jesus treated everyone, even those who disagreed with him, with respect and love. He attempted to win their allegiance through thoughtful dialogue, logical debate, storytelling and commonsense reasoning. He never argued anyone into the kingdom.

Reread the account of Jesus' encounter with the rich young ruler for an interesting apologetic approach. After the young man turned to walk away, Jesus did not violate the young man's integrity by ridiculing his decision or trying to coerce him to change his mind. He allowed him to refuse to believe.

While it's hard for us to understand, this is the highest form of love and respect. I fear some apologists enjoy the fray of the debate more than the grace of the gospel. If our evangelistic or apologetic approach offends the one we are trying to reach, what have we gained? No doubt the very truth of the gospel is offensive to some people. We cannot control the outcome of truth's actions; however, we can control our own offensiveness. Our gentleness and reverence toward those we hope to win to faith will reap great dividends in the long run.

Third, Jesus accepted people where they were and invited them to come where he was. Whether he was dealing with Simon Peter, the Samaritan woman who met him at the well, or one of the religious leaders, his evangelistic and apologetic approach was to meet them where they were physically, spiritually and emotionally. Jesus never forced belief or adherence to his will; he invited all who would believe to come freely and drink of the water of life he offered.

Finally, Jesus so believed his message that he was willing to die for it. That level of passion gains a hearing anywhere. Postmodern people long for authenticity and passion. They become sickened by shallow, diluted convictions. They are tired of religion that seems to exist as an end in itself, rather than a means to a higher end. They see through religion that exists for self-preservation. When we passionately share the gospel, offering Jesus Christ as the gentle and reverent answer to life's most complex problems, I can't help but believe people will listen. And some will even believe.

Truth for Postmoderns: Sermon Examples

The following sermon by John Killinger, a masterful preacher, shows how truth can be proclaimed even in a climate of relativism. As you read "What Is Truth? Or Shirley MacLaine, Meet the Master,"[1] watch how Killinger uses narrative to draw in the hearer. Early on he cuts to the core of the matter: "Anyone who gets caught up in the whirlpool of life in a foreign country begins to wonder about the nature of truth, and Pilate was no exception." By implication, we are no exception either.

Watch for how he juxtaposes the Jewish worldview to that of the Romans and Pilate. He shows that Pilate came from a culture awash in relativism. He then leads the hearer to see that the time in which we live is not unlike the first-century world. He also highlights modern realities, which are fading in a postmodern world: "Combined with the cocksure rationalism of the eighteenth century, [our culture offered] a balanced, sober way of looking at life and its meaning." The modern worldviews of Hobbes, Kant, Whitehead, Husserl and Heidegger are contrasted to that of Shirley MacLaine. The modern world collides with the postmodern world.

Another thing to look for is the way Killinger accepts that there is a subjective side of truth just as valid as the objective, measurable side—a very postmodern understanding of reality: "when our dreams and unconscious life are valued as highly as the tough-minded realism of everyday existence." He illustrates his point with three believable stories from real-life experiences.

After building his case, he shifts his attention, and that of his hearers, to Easter. Here is where he makes a strong apologetic claim for the truth of the gospel. Killinger's sermon is a fine example of apologetic preaching to a postmodern world.

What Is Truth? Or Shirley MacLaine, Meet the Master

John Killinger
John 18:28–28

"What is truth?" We have to sympathize with Pilate, don't we? He wasn't in an easy situation. He was a Roman politician far from home, set down in a strange culture. Perhaps he had been the secretary of a senator or the son of a local potentate and had been given preferment in foreign service. One didn't look gift horses in the mouth. But it had not been an easy adjustment. The distance from Rome was itself a problem; transportation and communication were not easy. His wife was probably unhappy, stuck off in that bizarre little land a month's sea-travel from her family and friends and the gossip of the Imperial City. The food and language weren't what they were accustomed to, nor were the people, with their extraordinary, fanatical religious customs.

Anyone who gets caught up in the whirlpool of life in a foreign country begins to wonder about the nature of truth, and Pilate was no exception. The Jews said there is one God; Pilate was accustomed to acknowledging many. The Jews had strict laws and customs from their God; Pilate's laws all came from the state, while his gods tended to disport themselves like spoiled children. The Jews kept to themselves to protect the purity of their race; Pilate had become a cosmopolitan, adapting to the scene where he lived. It is no wonder that when he became unintentionally involved in the trial of Jesus, which he regarded as a Jewish matter, he was puzzled and asked, "What is truth?" Under the circumstances, we would have wondered the same.

In fact, we often wonder today, don't we? We live, like Pilate, in a strange, sometimes bewildering world. Our parents, we fancy, didn't. Their world was smaller, tighter, more surely structured. They knew what they believed about everything. They had been taught by their parents and grandparents. Society reinforced their understanding of life and the world around them. If they wanted to know what they thought about something, they had but to consult the opinions bequeathed by an earlier generation.

A friend who owns a tenant farm in Kentucky told me this little story that illustrates the way it used to be for most of us. On a visit to the farm, he was walking about with the tenant, an old man from a rigid Pentecostalist background. The tenant's little blond-headed granddaughter, three or four years old, was running about with them. Whenever something contrary to the old man's way of thinking came up in the conversation, he made a point of saying, so the little girl could hear, "We don't believe in that, do we?" It was always the same, whether the subject was dancing, smoking, working on Sunday or giving equal rights to women: "We don't believe in that, do we?"

As the three of them approached the farm pond, they discovered that one of the ducks had hatched her eggs and was now surrounded by a dozen scurrying, cheeping balls of yellow fluff. The little girl ran to them and squatted in their midst. For a few moments she was entranced. Then, suddenly remembering herself, she looked up at her grandfather and said, "Granddaddy, do we beweeve in ducks?"

Her conditioning was almost complete.

So was ours, until a few years ago. Our white Anglo-Saxon Protestant culture, protected by our country's insularity, had easily maintained control of popular thinking. Combined with the cocksure rationalism of the eighteenth century, it was a balanced, sober way of looking at life and its meaning. God was in heaven, humankind was put on the earth to work hard and maintain order, prayer was a neat recitation of our common needs, and one simply didn't inquire into matters of mystery and metaphysics. The afterlife was divided into heaven and hell, and any thirst for knowledge beyond that was deemed akin to witchcraft and devil worship.

But the first truly global war in the history of the world, with the enormous tran-
scultural migrations it produced, plus the growth of modern travel and the development of television and an era of instant communication, changed all that, didn't it?
A generation of American young people began going to India and Tibet to study
Buddhist meditation. Well-to-do natives in Pango Pango began importing Japanese
TV sets and American air conditioners. Beatlemania encircled the globe. Llama
rugs from Bolivia and Peru were sold at roadside stands in Georgia and Alabama.
Teenagers in Greenland, Italy and Korea went crazy over blue jeans. Primitive
dances in Borneo and Zimbabwe were shown on television screens all over the
Western Hemisphere. Centuries-old worldviews and belief structures began to
crumble. We all found ourselves asking Pilate's question, "What is truth?"

We're still asking, more often than ever.

After hundreds of years of a great philosophical tradition, from Thomas Hobbes
and Immanuel Kant to Whitehead and Husserl and Heidegger, Shirley MacLaine is
the most talked-about thinker of our time. Her book *Out on a Limb*, with its descrip-
tions of séances, out-of-body experiences and channeling, has become a runaway
bestseller among people who sense that the wholeness of truth lies beyond the conventional little systems most of us grew up with and that, even if MacLaine is a kind
of lovable kook, she is toying with a dimension of human existence as real and significant as mainline Protestantism, the Mona Lisa and the Dow Jones Average.

Recent surveys show that the percentage of people in America who admit to
having had ESP, extraterrestrial, life-after-life, out-of-body or reincarnation experiences has shot up from 40 percent ten years ago to about 75 percent today. Think of
that: three out of four Americans professing to have had superphenomenal experiences, experiences that cannot be subsumed under the old classifications of religion
and reality.

Does that mean that the nature of reality has drastically changed in our lifetime?
Does it means that the end of the world is approaching? No. It means that the old
ways of thinking and perceiving are breaking down. We are shedding some of our
straitjackets. We are more open to a variety of visions and perceptions than our parents and grandparents. We understand something about the extraordinary versatility
of truth. We are entering a period predicted by André Breton, the remarkable surre-
alist, when our dreams and unconscious life are valued as highly as the tough-
minded realism of everyday existence.

A woman who lived alone went to bed in the upstairs of her large house. In the
middle of the night, she was awakened by a dream of her long-dead mother, who
told her to get up; there was danger in the basement. Slipping on her robe, the

woman descended to the basement and found a fire just starting in some old papers near the water heater.

A splendid young Air Force chaplain I met in Japan had begun his military career as a nineteen-year-old marine in Vietnam. One day, as he was entering the restroom of his barracks, a great pain struck him in his side, knocking him to the floor. Gasping for breath, he dragged himself across the floor and pulled up to the sink. Later he learned that his father in Georgia had been thrown from a car wreck and was killed at precisely the same moment the pain had struck him. This incredible moment of sympathetic pain became a key element in the young man's decision to study for the ministry.

A businessman in Washington, D.C., was "killed" on a bridge when his car skidded on wet pavement; he later wrote the story of it himself. When it happened, he said, it was as if everything was occurring in slow motion. He felt himself being thrown from his body, and for several minutes he hovered a few feet above the scene of the accident. He watched the police and medics arrive and saw them working over his body. He felt completely serene and joyous; in fact, he had never felt so good in his whole life. Then he heard a voice calling him back to his body. He resisted; he didn't want to return. "You still have much to do," said the voice. Reluctantly, he went back.

The medics were startled, for they had found no pulse or heartbeat and were sure he was dead. His whole life was reoriented by the experience. Now, he says, he is loving and generous; he never becomes anxious about the things that once troubled him; and his entire existence has become "beautifully religious."

What is truth? We dare not draw the circle too small, do we?

So we swarm to church on Easter to pay homage to One who rose from the dead—or supposedly rose from the dead. That's what our faith teaches, isn't it? Perhaps it's the one place where our narrow old faith and the wild new world of speculation converge. They agree on the possibility and provide a double reason for our being here.

Maybe we don't all come very often, for we're not convinced. But on Easter something draws us—something primordial, immemorial; something instinctive; something that says, "This mystery lies at the heart of all life, even all truth."

What if we reoriented our lives around it? I mean, suppose it is true that Christ rose from the dead, that the tomb was empty and Jesus appeared to his disciples in spectral form, that Christianity has been proclaiming the truth all these years, that God was in Christ showing us the nature of reality and inviting us to a new way of seeing everything. What would happen if we restructured our entire existence around this truth, made it the linchpin of everything we believed and did in the future?

What if Shirley MacLaine were to come face to face with the Master? It would be the best proof she ever had, wouldn't it, that the spirit world is as real as the physical world? She would see love as the primary modality for all true and lasting action. She would experience herself as belonging to God, the way Mary Magdalene did that first Easter in the garden when she fell at Christ's feet crying, "Rabboni! Rabboni! Master!" She would see the whole future in terms of the kingdom of God, and begin to serve that kingdom with a fervor that would surprise even her. And she would never, never again be afraid of death.

That's the way it would be for us. Our lives would be completely transformed. Nothing would ever be the same again.

I remember a professor of philosophy I knew when I was in graduate school. He had studied in Holland and Sweden and Great Britain as well as in America, pursuing truth with the finest minds in the world. There was nothing he liked better than to pore over old books and argue with their authors. He was a brilliant man, and his head was filled with postulates and systems and ideas. He had been an agnostic, suspending commitment to any final system of thought lest it hamper him in his exploration of other systems. But he told of an experience he had when his second child was only a few months old. She fell ill with a high fever, and the doctor put her in the hospital. The mother was exhausted, and the father urged her to go home and get some sleep while he stayed in the room with the child.

"I was sitting there feeling so helpless," he said. "My mind raced from one thing to another, from this idea to the other. Finally, when I thought I would go crazy with worry and grief, I began thinking the words of an old hymn I must have learned when I was a boy: 'O Jesus, I have promised to serve thee to the end.'

"Over and over I sang them in my head, until finally I found myself singing them aloud. I got down on my knees by my daughter's bed and I prayed, 'O Lord, Truth with a capital T.' "

Before he got up, he committed himself to Christ again, and then committed his little daughter to God's care. During the night her fever broke, and two days later she was able to leave the hospital. "But even if she had died," he said, "I believe I would have remained committed to Christ. I learned that night that there isn't any truth apart from him."

That's the way it was with Pilate, wasn't it? He began by asking, "What is truth?" And then, after he had been with Jesus for a little while, had spoken with Jesus and observed his behavior under enormous pressure, he saw that truth somehow had its dwelling place in this strangely dignified and otherworldly man. Jesus' enemies had accused him of posing as the king of the Jews and trying to start a rebellion against Rome. They brought pressure on Pilate to commit him to death by crucifixion. But Pilate had the last word. When they took Jesus off to Golgotha, the site of execution, he sent them with a sign to put over His head. It said, "Jesus of Nazareth, King of the Jews."

"Don't write 'The King of the Jews,' " said the chief priests; "write, 'This man said, I am King of the Jews.' "

"What I have written," said Pilate, "I have written."

Pilate knew he had come face to face with the Truth. Jesus was truly a king.

Unfortunately, Pilate didn't restructure his life around his discovery.

Perhaps we shall do better.

In Summary

Apologetic preaching to the postmodern world means taking seriously the multiple understandings of reality held by people today. Because there is no notion of absolute truth within postmodernism, Christian faith becomes one option among many. This chapter has focused on how preachers can address the postmodern world without compromising the essence of the gospel of Jesus Christ. John Killinger's sermon shows that it is possible to preach truth in a climate of relativism.

Having dealt with the issue of truth, we can move to the next chapter with the question, Is it possible to preach Jesus Christ to a postmodern world?

6

Proclaiming Jesus Christ to a Postmodern World

BECAUSE CHRISTIAN THEOLOGY REMAINS OBVIOUSLY CHRIST-centered, a homiletic theology must ultimately deal with preaching Jesus Christ not only in but to a postmodern world. This chapter focuses on the life of Jesus Christ as God's quintessential act of self-revelation to the world.

Who is Jesus of Nazareth? Is Jesus Christ the Son of God? What does it mean for Jesus to be Savior of the world? How does God reconcile the world to himself through Jesus Christ? Did Jesus Christ have to die? What role does Jesus Christ play in the world today? Are such questions even necessary? Is anyone asking questions like this today? With the Christian faith under attack from within through books like John Spong's *Why Christianity Must Change or Die*,[1] church leaders cannot avoid dealing with questions like these. Answering these questions becomes the paramount task of apologetic preaching, both to the church and out of the church to the world. This chapter offers theological groundwork and method for preaching Jesus Christ to a postmodern world.

What we know about Jesus Christ—biographically, historically and theologically—comes to us in the New Testament. The New Testament writers were biographers, historians and apologists with a theological goal. I would dare say that one cannot find pure history—that is *history for history's sake*—in the entire Bible. Certainly one will not find it in the New Testament. The writers of the New Testament were primarily concerned with theology; first and foremost, they were theologians. One could say they were preachers first and historians second. History and biography were tools by which they made their theological claims.

The Gospel writers used narrative as the vehicle to paint their theological portraits of Jesus. A former seminary colleague used to ask his students, "Which would you rather have, the Gospels or an unedited videotape of Jesus' life?" Because they grew up in a video culture, the students' first impulse was to jump quickly to the conclusion that a videotape would be absolutely wonderful. At long last, they would get to see what Jesus and the disciples *really* looked like. They could see the landscape of Galilee, the wilderness where Satan tempted Jesus, and Jerusalem as it was when Jesus taught there. They could view the miracles and signs as they occurred. Finally they could see what happened at the tomb that first Easter morning. They would get a glimpse of Jesus ascending into heaven. With a videotape, many of their questions would be answered. Doubt could be erased completely—or so they conjectured.

Since my professor friend was a New Testament scholar, you know the answer to his question was not "a videotape." However, he had the students right where he wanted them. We know the New Testament is not a sterile chronological record of Jesus' life. The New Testament, inspired by God, represents a theological recounting of Jesus' life and times. The writers' goal was to proclaim Jesus as God's full revelation of himself to humankind. They were not interested in merely providing an accounting of Jesus' life for posterity's sake. They had no interest in presenting a first-century travelogue about Jesus' world. Presenting the truth of who Jesus was and why he came was their ultimate aim.

That's why Luke begins his Gospel stating a theological purpose. He mentions the fulfillment of events and the need for Theophilus to know the truth about the instruction he has received. Here, implicitly, Luke lays out his historical-theological underpinnings—foretold events were fulfilled in Jesus' life, and one can know truth. John's Gospel states the writer's theological goal explicitly: "Now Jesus did many other signs in the presence of his disciples, which are not written in this book. But these are written so that you may come to believe that Jesus is the Messiah, the Son of God, and that through believing you may have life in his name" (Jn 20:30–31). John's purpose was not merely to provide an account of Jesus' life for the sake of history. His was a theological purpose: to generate belief that Jesus was the promised Messiah, the Son of God, and that through believing in Christ, his hearers would have eternal life.

Again, the Gospel writers used narrative to paint their portraits of Jesus. Matthew, Mark and Luke each have a different theological goal in mind. Therefore their pictures of Jesus differ. John's Gospel presents a chronology much different from the Synoptics because one of his theological purposes is to show that Jesus replaces the temple. So no wonder John's Gospel begins with Jesus cleansing the temple—an event that comes chronologically late in the Synoptics. The portraits we see in the Gospels come to us as stories serving an intentional theological end.

The other writings of the New Testament provide theological reflection on Jesus Christ through direct discourse. In letters written to specific churches facing particular circumstances, the New Testament writers reflected on Jesus' life and how it should inform the ethics, values and practices of the churches. Whether sermonically—as in James and Hebrews—or through extended debate and discourse—as in Romans and 1 and 2 Corinthians—the writers express themselves theologically. Their ultimate end is to make theological claims—evangelistically and apologetically—on behalf of Jesus Christ. They offer Jesus Christ as the fullness of God's revelation to humankind. Community life was transformed as the churches yielded themselves to the teaching of Jesus through the ministries of the apostles and other New Testament writers.

Why are these issues important in a discussion about preaching Jesus

Christ to a postmodern world? Remember from earlier discussions, post-modernism is skeptical of things that appear to be inauthentic; authenticity is a critical desire of postmodernism. If one does not fully understand the nature of the New Testament, one could presume that it is fraught with problems and contradictions. An example already mentioned is the chronology of the temple cleansing in the Synoptics compared to the Gospel of John. A thoughtful postmodern reader could argue that these different chronologies constitute a contradiction. Either the Synoptics are correct in placing the event near the close of Jesus' public ministry, or John is correct placing it as one of Jesus' inaugural acts. A close reading of the account—without an understanding of the New Testament's composition—could result in a charge of contradiction.

While some biblical scholars might argue for two temple cleansings, most account for the apparent problem in chronology a different way. They presume the Synoptic Gospels describe the truer historical chronology of the event. John does not attempt a historical recounting but a theological telling of the story; hence his freedom in reordering the event to highlight his theological intent. In other words, John is a theologian using narrative discourse as his way of teaching theology. That John is convinced that certain events actually happened is not debatable; but he chose to retell the events in such a way as to highlight certain theological truths. The point I am making remains: effective proclamation of Jesus Christ in a postmodern epoch must emerge from a correct theological understanding of its source materials, namely the New Testament.

Jesus of Nazareth

A monograph written several years ago titled *Preaching Jesus Christ* bemoans the widespread misunderstandings of Jesus that were being propagated from American pulpits. The author's concern centered on how people subjectively interpret Jesus according to their immediate personal needs and presuppositions. If your bent is psychology, then Jesus looks like the great therapist. If you lean toward social action, Jesus becomes the divine social activist. If you are a feminist, Jesus sounds a lot like the keynote speaker for the National Organization for Women. If you are an evangelical, Jesus becomes the local director of Promise Keepers.

Tex Sample, in his book *U.S. Lifestyles and Mainline Churches*, agrees that American Christians have a tendency to view Jesus in extremely accommodating terms: "Sallman's head of Christ turned Jesus into an Anglo with movie-star looks. Bruce Barton's *The Man Nobody Knows* made Jesus a Rotarian. . . . The New Age makes him a channeler, a guru, or a guide. Athletes turn him into a jock, and rock lovers proclaim him a superstar."[2] The author of *All God's Children and Blue Suede Shoes* has problems with Christians who incorporate cultural images by merely sanitizing them with "Jesus language."[3] In an attempt to be culturally relevant to the Coca-Cola generation, Jesus becomes "the Real Thing." The list could go on.

If we are to be effective in the pulpit, we must hold our biases at bay. Otherwise Jesus begins to look a lot like our wishes and desires. In *Your God Is Too Small*, J. B. Phillips warned that when God becomes a projected image of our own personal morality, we wind up merely worshiping ourselves.[4] And if we learn anything about Jesus from the New Testament, we know that he never fit into neat categories, religious or otherwise.

When we read the Gospel accounts of Jesus' life, we need to be careful that we don't ask questions that were not issues to the writers. Preachers are not immune to such hermeneutical mistakes. We should come to the Gospel texts with openness, allowing them to speak without reading into them our wishes about what we want them to say. Hans-Georg Gadamer in *Truth and Method*—his magnum opus on hermeneutics—warns interpreters to avoid projecting a premature understanding of meaning onto a text.[5] He says that too often as soon as we begin to think we understand a text, we make huge leaps of *prognosis*—that is, presuming a foreknowledge of the text's meaning. All too often such leaps yield faulty interpretations because the text is not allowed to speak; the interpreter's presuppositions shout too loudly. Such a caution is more easily expressed than carried out, because the material in the Gospels is so familiar to those of us who preach.

The Illusion of the First Time

One way to interpret the Gospels is to try to create an *illusion of the first time* as you read, study and preach them. The idea of the illusion of the first time comes from stage theater. Actors have to create for the audience the illusion that what is happening on stage is actually happening for the first time as the audience watches it. The audience is supposed to be transported in time and space to events taking place on stage as though these events had never happened before.

An actor opens a door into a dark room, steps in and turns on a light. A woman's body, covered in blood, lies sprawled over a couch. The entering actor sees the body and screams in shock and fear. The audience becomes caught up in the moment.

Who has been duped? The audience, of course. The actor who screamed knew the body would be sprawled over the couch. He's seen it sprawled over the couch in the last one hundred performances and through numerous rehearsals before that. What happens is that actors create the illusion that what the audience sees is happening new and fresh—for the first time. Hence the *illusion of the first time.*

A fresh reading of the New Testament is possible for those who preach if we will attempt to come to it as though it is were first time we had read or heard the stories. In other words, we should attempt to have an illusion of the first time as we read the Bible. This is easier said than done, yet it is possible nonetheless. By allowing texts to speak again for themselves, we will find that they yield fresh insights.

One cardinal sin of many preachers and interpreters is to run too quickly to commentaries to hear the words of the experts. When you do this, the text tends to speak only through the filter of the commentator. I like to remind myself to stay away from the commentaries for a time, to read and hear the text for myself.

I often read the text aloud, in several different translations, trying to hear the tone and timbre of the writer's heart. Listen to the text with all your senses. What do you *hear* as you read? Do you hear the sound of sheep grazing along the River Jordan? Do you hear the cacophonous crowd entering the temple? What do you *smell* as you read? Do you smell the multifarious odors of the marketplace? Do you smell the fish in Peter's boat? What do you *feel* tactilely as you read? Can you feel the garment Jesus wears as the woman grabs hold of it? Do you feel the push of those sitting in the house as the paralyzed man is lowered to Jesus by his friends? What do you *see* as you read? Can you see the Sea of Galilee as storm winds brew? Do you see the Israelites gathered before the Red Sea? What do you *taste* as you read? Can you taste the fish Jesus prepared for Peter's breakfast? Do you taste the cool water Jesus drank at the well in Samaria? A new appreciation for the richness of the Bible will emerge when you read with all of your senses engaged. You will come away from the text with a fresh understanding.

Another way to create the illusion of the first time is to ask yourself questions like these: What would I think if I were reading this story for the very first time? Would I be shocked, surprised, worried, confounded? If I had never read or heard this passage before, what would bother me about it? What would excite me about it? What would trouble me about it? Does the text call into question some things I've always believed but now, having read this text, have to reconsider? Coming to the text with fresh eyes and ears, am I seeing a different picture of Jesus? How does this picture differ from the one I used to bring to the New Testament? Asking questions like these will help you create a fresh encounter with the text. Reading the New Testament with an *illusion of the first time* will help to yield a fresh understanding of these sacred stories.

Now when you open the Gospels and begin reading about Jesus, the young man from the city of Nazareth, you will find that your presuppositions about who he is and what he did will be more freshly formed. When we read the New Testament and allow it to speak, we find that our turn-of-the-millennium notions of Jesus and his motivations no longer make sense. We are left with the challenge of dealing with a Jesus whose culture and upbringing shaped him socially and theologically. When we read Luke's account of young Jesus in the temple (Lk 2:41–52), we should be less apt to impose a contemporary psychological reading. We should ask, beyond the above questions, Why does Luke tell us this about Jesus? How does this account of Jesus' life help us understand Jesus theologically? Another interesting question might be, why does Luke include this account while none of the other writers think it important to include in their stories of Jesus? For example, the account of the two disciples who fail to recognize Jesus on the road to Emmaus is found only in Luke. Why did Luke think this story important? Does the answer to that question help us better understand Luke's intention and purpose?

There has always been a quest for the historical Jesus of Nazareth, as though if we really knew what he did and really knew what he looked like—if we had a videotape—we would be better served as Christians and believers. The Gospels offer us a theological glimpse into the mind of God by laying out for us the life of One born to poor parents in a hamlet called Nazareth, who grew in the wisdom and knowledge of God, who carried out a ministry of healing and teaching, who was outcast for his radical views, who saw the religion of the day as oppressive, who died on a Roman cross, who rose from the dead, and who appeared to those he loved to offer them hope and challenge them to be his followers in the world. The point of the matter: the writers painted pictures of the Nazarene as they did not so we could have a reconstruction of the historical Jesus, but so we could see Jesus as the Christ, the Son of the living God.

Jesus the Christ

At Caesarea Philippi Jesus asked his disciples, "Who do people say that I am?" Probably this was an easy question for them to answer. Jesus was certainly talked about in the circles the disciples frequented. Their reply: Some people were saying Jesus was one of the prophets, even the prophet

Elijah. Others said he was John the Baptist come back to life.

Then came the haunting question that forced the disciples to come to grips with their own view of Jesus. Jesus asked, "Who do you say that I am?"

Peter's response eventually became a confession for the early church: "You are the Christ, the Son of the living God."

What did Peter mean when he called Jesus the Messiah—the Christ, the Anointed One of God? What did Peter mean theologically? What did Peter mean in terms of his own understanding of Jesus? What does it mean for us today to call Jesus the Christ of God? In many ways it's easier to formulate questions than to come up with answers. Though we easily talk to postmodern people about Jesus of Nazareth, speaking of Jesus as the Christ becomes more difficult. Even Peter's confession was fraught with misunderstanding, as a continued reading of the Gospel accounts reveals. The reason for the difficulty lies in the exclusive claim implicit in seeing Jesus as God's Anointed One, as the Christ. Such exclusive claims are difficult to hear in politically correct postmodernism. Yet if we are to be faithful to the gospel, we must not allow our concern about a difficult hearing to keep us from offering the news that we understand as God's hope for the world—the postmodern world included.

The mystery of the incarnation—the doctrine that describes Jesus as fully human and fully divine—is the turning point of history in Christian theology. God's wisdom dictated that to understand humanity fully, God had to become human. In my previous work on identification and preaching I described the incarnation as the ultimate example of God's identification with the real humanity of real people. As Jesus walked, lived, slept, ate, laughed, died and rose again, so went God. God exists not as a distant landlord insulated from the anxieties of human life but as the One who has lived and now lives to offer real life. Authentic life—purposeful, joy-filled, Christ-centered—is a wonderful possibility in postmodern times because God incarnate understands postmodernism too.

This divine-human Jesus—the divine entering into human history—remains the center of the good news we preach, its beginning and end. The ultimate aim of apologetic preaching is to proclaim such hope as the viable alternative to the relativism of the current age. Jesus Christ answers skepticism and doubt about humanity's ultimate progress by offering good news.

Postmodernism's misunderstanding of Christianity remains an obstacle. An *authentic* reading of the Gospels and a focused theology wrapped around Jesus of Nazareth, the Christ, breaks open the false notion that Christianity is narrow-minded and oppressive. For a society looking for liberation, Jesus Christ—God with us—remains the liberating answer. Christianity is not just another religion or altruistic faith system. It is based on God's good news that in Christ, God makes life available to all who would believe (Jn 3:16).

The hope for postmoderns rests in John's proclamation "And the Word became flesh and lived among us" (Jn 1:14). Jesus Christ is where the subjective and objective converge. Ultimately Jesus provides the bridge between modernism and postmodernism, in that he is both objective (an actual person who lived and acted in history) and subjective (he is in fact a person of feelings and emotions who has a story to tell and whose story we must tell and involve ourselves in). Thus it's important not to reject the postmodern emphasis on the subjective in favor of the modern emphasis on the objective. Instead we can emphasize that in the Christian faith—in particular in Jesus—there is both. Our apologetic preaching to postmoderns must encompass both. And we continue to heed Peter's admonition: "Always be ready to make your defense to anyone who demands from you an accounting for the hope that is in you; yet do it with gentleness and reverence" (1 Pet 3:15–16).

Preaching Jesus Christ: Sermon Example

The following sermon is an example of proclaiming Jesus Christ to a postmodern world. You will recognize the introduction to the sermon. It is a reformulation of the opening part of this book. I use it here to show its homiletic use in preaching to a congregation.

The story sets the apologetic context. In my opinion, too many preachers and too many Christians opt for an easy approach to Christianity. They have sold the gospel short and are unwilling to hold fast to the gospel's exclusive demands or take a hard stand for the gospel. Too many Christian make apologies for God and act as if they are ashamed of the gospel. This sermon on Romans 16:1–2 addresses the issue.

Look for ways the sermon highlights the issues facing all Christians as we move into a new millennium—fear of becoming too big, fear of sounding like a fundamentalist, fear of sounding like a liberal, fear of being labeled narrow-minded. These fears, or fears like them, keep Christians from being faithful and effective witnesses. The introduction of the sermon tries to set the stage for us to grow beyond such fears. Following, the main thrust of the sermon is to hold up Paul's admonition as the model for us all to follow. We should not be ashamed of the gospel of Jesus Christ. Jesus is the subject and object of our faith and our preaching. The sermon attempts to model such an unashamed stance.

The closing illustration from Joseph Girzone provides a glimpse of what happens when the name of Jesus is held high. Girzone's approach provides a example of the power that the story of Jesus still has for people today. In a time when even Christian theologians are questioning the veracity of the accounts about Christ, this simple story reminds us that proclaiming Jesus still has transforming power. Apologetically, the sermon does set forth an account for the hope that we have. I believe it does so with gentleness and reverence. May Christ be glorified.

Not Ashamed

Romans 1:16–17

The book of Romans is Paul's most elaborate and in-depth theological statement. If you're ever unsure about its meaning, read chapter 1, verses 16 and 17—the theme, the heart, the essence of the entire book. Paul writes, "For I am not ashamed of the gospel; it is the power of God for salvation to everyone who has faith, to the Jew first and also to the Greek. For in it the righteousness of God is revealed through faith for faith; as it is written, 'The one who is righteous will live by faith.' "

On my office door I used to post a cartoon that showed a pastor seated at a large wooden desk. A church member was seated next to the desk. The pastor had a discouraged look on his face. His discouragement was probably based on the sign hanging on the wall behind him. The sign was a worship attendance chart that showed a steady decline in worship attendance for the past two years. It was obvious that in the next few months, the line would fall beyond the boundaries of the chart.

In an attempt to alleviate the pastor's despair, the member is saying to the pastor, in a caring and compassionate way, "You know, I'm no expert. But maybe you shouldn't close each sermon with 'But then again, what do I know?' "

The minister's despair shows us a little bit about the anxiety that is facing ministers and churches in their work today. We live and minister and worship and work between times. The dogmatism of yesterday's pulpits has given way to ambivalence in modern pulpits. In the face of political correctness on one side and the fear of sounding like a rabid fundamentalist on the other, preachers skulk from their studies wide-eyed and confused, like children on their first day of school.

What are we preachers so afraid of? Where's the basis for our fear? We fear successful megachurches, which are doing a great job at marketing their programs and drawing baby busters and baby boomers and Gen Xers from all over the community and, yes, even from our own churches. We fear that if we push too hard or press too much, it won't work. We fear that if we don't push hard enough and press hard enough, it won't work. We fear being labeled narrow-minded by the media, our colleagues, our neighbors and even our own church members. Words like *sin, judgment, righteousness, immoral* and *evil* are words that we are so afraid to use today. You know what happens, don't you? If we use them, we may offend someone's sensibilities. We might make someone mad. And God forbid that you ever make a church member mad!

We fear being labeled with the religious right, and we fear being labeled with the religious left. We are so hypercautious that our sermons at best offend no one and at worst bore our listeners altogether. We fear being too successful, but we fear the alternative even more.

And with all of that fear we come into the pulpit apologizing for God. Oh, we're really sorry that we have to talk about the cross. We are really sorry that we would dare say to our people that they're supposed to love their enemies. We come into the pulpit apologizing for God because we are afraid if we don't somehow temper the gospel, if we don't make it a little easier for people to swallow, if we don't water it down a little bit, the pews will be empty.

And as I think about it—as I think about us standing in this moment in time, getting ready to move into the third millennium—as I think about all the things that are out there from which we can find fear, I think Dorothy is right, "We're not in Kansas anymore, Toto."

Yet in the midst of our hesitancy and our cowardly silence and the commitment to secular motives that mars our discipleship, we hear the words of Paul echoing in our ears: "For I am not ashamed of the gospel; it is the power of God for salvation to everyone who would believe, to the Jew first and also to the Greek. For in it is revealed the righteousness of God from faith to faith; as it is written, 'The just [or the righteous] shall live by faith.' "

Paul says, "I am not ashamed of the gospel. Oh, there may be some things I am ashamed about. I'm ashamed of my background; I'm ashamed of where I've been; I'm ashamed of what I've done; but I will tell you one thing—I'm not ashamed of the gospel."

Think about the background from which Paul writes. He had been in prison in Philippi. He had been chased out of Thessalonica. He had been laughed at in Athens. In Corinth the Greeks thought he was a fool, and the Jews thought his message was a stumblingblock to faith. And in the midst of all that—all the difficulty, all the craziness that Paul faced—he says, "I'm not ashamed of the gospel. I'm not ashamed of it, and I will proclaim it no matter what happens."

Paul echoes Jesus' sentiments. In Mark's Gospel, Jesus says, "Those who are ashamed of me and of my words in this adulterous and sinful generation, of them the Son of Man will also be ashamed when he comes in the glory of his Father" (Mk 8:38). And again in Luke's Gospel: "Those who are ashamed of me and of my words, of them the Son of Man will be ashamed when He comes in his glory and the glory of the Father and of the holy angels" (Lk 9:26). Paul continues the ministry of Jesus Christ by saying, "I am not ashamed of the gospel."

Paul also recognized that at his time in history, people really needed to hear good news. People needed to have something in which to anchor their faith. People needed something to hold on to.

Doesn't that sound like contemporary America? People are reaching and grasping at straws to find hope and to make sense of their lives. They grab a little thing here, they search for some meaning there. We are told if we do this, we'll be happy. And guess what? We do it and we're still miserable. And they tell us if we just have this product, we'll be set for life. Did you ever notice how often TV commercials tell you what you should have? Have this. Have that. Do this. Do that. But the gospel says, if you really want happiness, if you really want fullness, Jesus Christ will fill you where there's emptiness, will touch you where there's a lack of anything.

Paul says, "I am not ashamed of the gospel; it is the power of God for salvation." The Greek word used here for "power" is *dynamis*. From that word we get an English word. Do you know what it is? *Dynamite*. The power of God, the dynamite of God that will explode things in a positive way. Salvation is by the power of God.

Paul is clear that salvation is not just a moment when you get your salvation card punched, and then later in heaven you show it to God and say, "See, here it is—my salvation card—so let me in." Paul makes it clear that salvation is a process, a pilgrimage, a walk, a journey. Paul says in other places, "You were saved; you are being saved; you will be saved." It is a process; it's a journey; it's a life of growth.

But I wonder, what are we saved from or for? Well, throughout the book of Romans, Paul gives us several hints. One of the things we are saved from is physical illness. Hm, that sounds rather strange. You say, "Wait a minute. I know people who are saved and are still sick." But you know what happens with physical illness? It sometimes debilitates our spirit. It breaks apart our spirit and causes us to wonder what is going on and where God is. The salvation Paul is talking about is so much bigger than physical illnesses. It is a recognition that we are not just made up of flesh and blood. There's more to our lives. We are bigger than that.

It's also salvation from danger. Paul is one who has been through everything. He was shipwrecked, snake bitten, beat up, thrown around, stoned, and yet he realized that in Christ all his suffering meant nothing. There was no danger in Christ; in Christ all danger was gone.

It's also salvation from modern life's infection. If you are not careful as a Christian, the culture in which you live will infect you. It will infect you with greed. It will infect you with jealousy. It will infect you with envy. The culture in which we live will infect you with the ways of the world. It will infect you with the way relationships are done outside the church. The culture in which we live will infect you with all kinds of things. But in Jesus Christ you have an inoculation to help protect you from that infection.

Paul would also say that you are saved from lostness. If you are lost, you are on a road outside of Jesus Christ, and that road is going nowhere. But if you are with Christ, saved, you are on a road that Jesus Christ has laid out before you. And Jesus Christ walks with you every step of that way.

You are saved from sin. You are saved from judgment—because Jesus Christ has already experienced judgment on your behalf. It's over. It's done. It's finished. It is finished! Where have you heard that before?

Paul says, "I am not ashamed of the gospel; it is the power of God for salvation

to all who have faith, to the Jew first and also to the Greek. For in it the righteousness of God is revealed"—is made known by God (and I like the next four words,
it's the crux of everything Paul writes about)—"through faith for faith." Or trans-
lated "faith alone," or "from God's faithfulness to our faith." I like that. From God's
faithfulness in Christ to our own faith.

What Paul is talking about here is not just "belief in." Sometimes we think, *Oh,*
I have faith in someone. Or, *I believe them.* But Paul's not talking about just belief.
It's not just head knowledge. The faith that Paul calls us to have is an overwhelming
acceptance and trust that Christ knows best for us. It's an overwhelming belief that
our faith is given to Christ. It is betting our life, as one writer has said, on Jesus
Christ. I like what another writer said, "It means being totally sold out for Jesus."

I want Immanuel Baptist Church to be a church that is totally sold out for
Jesus. That there is no will that is our will. That there is no place that is your
place. That there is no place that is my place. I want us to be so sold out for Jesus
Christ that when people come into this place on Sunday mornings, they don't see
you, they don't see me, they don't see the choir. They see Jesus. We need to be so
sold out for Jesus Christ, Paul says, that it becomes his will—nothing more, nothing less, nothing else. Sold out for Christ. This is what the world needs; and one
reason the church is not making a dent in the closing years of the second millennium and the beginning of the third millennium is that we are sold out to ourselves rather than being sold out to Jesus Christ. When we are sold out to Jesus
Christ, having the faith that is from faith to faith—then we wind up worshiping a
God of righteousness.

There are ramifications to worshiping a God of righteousness. The first is that
because God is righteous, because God is so utterly holy, we know that God is not
arbitrary. God is not cruel. He's going to deal with us in mercy and in love. We also
have an ethical responsibility placed upon our lives, because the righteousness of
God is to be lived out in your right way of living and my right way of living.

It all boils down to Paul saying, "I am not ashamed of the gospel." What needs
to happen now is that you and I need to go out from here and start telling people
about Jesus. We must stand on that truth and not water it down one iota. Because if
we water it down, we might as well stay home. It is not your intellect that will save
you. It is not technology. I am not ashamed of the gospel of Jesus Christ, because it
is the core and heartbeat of all that we are. And here is an opportunity for us to be
about kingdom issues as Jesus Christ molds and makes us after his will.

Some of you may know Joseph Girzone. You may have heard of him. He is the
author of the Joshua novels. Girzone was invited to Sanford University to take part

in a weeklong lecture series there on Christ and the arts. He was supposed to be the first speaker.

Girzone got up, and of course, being the first speaker, he could have tried to set the agenda for the week. He could have laid out what he thought was the most important thing. He could have shared all of the great things that he had done, his pedigree and all of that stuff. But in that great hall packed with people—the last three or four rows of people had to stand—Girzone leaves the platform and begins walking among the people. As he walks, he's talking in a rather quiet voice, but loud enough for everyone to hear. And he begins talking about Jesus. He walks around those people, not saying anything different from what anyone else had ever said about Jesus. Repeating the same story that has been repeated a thousand million times, just walking through that crowd talking about Jesus. John Killinger, who reported the event, said, "His speech was simple, direct, without embellishment. And yet everyone said afterwards that it was one of the highlights of their lives, that something miraculous had happened in that auditorium, that you could feel the presence living and breathing there."[6]

We don't need to tell people about Immanuel Baptist Church. We don't need to tell people about our Sunday school or our music program. We need to be talking about Jesus, about how Jesus came to earth, was found in a manger and grew up in a Jewish family but pressed himself to know God and to love God. And that when Jesus would come into a crowd, he made everybody there feel special. Nobody felt like an outsider. Nobody felt like they weren't allowed to be there. Nobody looked down at their clothes and thought, *Boy! I shouldn't be here today.* Jesus would come into a crowd and everybody would feel welcome. And he spread that throughout the world in which he lived. And he ultimately was nailed to a cross because of kindness. And he was crucified because he loved too much. And he died because you and I are sinners.

We should talk about Jesus. And we should be able to say to the world, "I am not ashamed of the gospel, because it is the power of God for salvation for all who would believe."

When you leave here today, and you go to a restaurant, do me a favor. Don't talk about worship; talk about Jesus. Don't talk about your Sunday school; talk about Jesus. Don't talk about somebody else; talk about Jesus. If you and I leave here talking about Jesus, the world will be changed forever. Now that's nothing to be ashamed about!

In Summary

A pastor was giving a children's sermon. He said to the kids, "I'm going to describe something, and I want you to guess what I'm talking about.

"It's small and gray," he began. "It has a bushy tail. It climbs trees." You could see the children's minds racing.

The pastor continued, "During the summer it finds nuts and stores them for the winter." At this point one little boy jumped to his feet, hand waving wildly in the air. He knew the answer.

"Okay, Robbie," said the pastor, "what am I talking about?"

Robbie responded, "Well, I know the answer's Jesus, but it sure sounds like a squirrel to me!"

When it comes to apologetic preaching, we know the final answer is going to be Jesus. However, in practice, preaching Jesus Christ to and within a postmodern context becomes more difficult. With many presuppositions about Christian faith being called into question, even by people within the Christian community, the significance of faithful and apologetic proclamation of Jesus as God's ultimate revelation to humankind cannot be overstated.

This chapter has attempted to develop a foundation on which we can faithfully proclaim Jesus Christ to our postmodern world. The next and final chapter addresses some practical matters to keep in mind as we preach apologetic sermons.

7

How to Apologize Without Saying You're Sorry

MY GOAL IN WRITING THIS BOOK WAS TO PRESENT A PRACTICAL homiletic theology for apologetic preaching. I agree with the sentiment attributed to Karl Barth: theology that cannot be preached remains worthless to the church. Theology should uplift, inform and edify believers. Mere philosophical talk about God that does not intersect the real lives of real people becomes an academic exercise. Theology should help the people in the pew view the world *Godward*. In other words, theology should help them see where God is working in the world, in their lives, in the circumstances that beset them.

Because preaching is a practical theology discipline, this chapter addresses the pragmatic matters of apologetic preaching. Topics to be covered include apologetic topics and themes, developing a scheduled plan for apologetic preaching, apologetic preaching and evangelism, apologetic preaching to the church, and planning worship services with apologetic emphases.

Apologetic Topics and Themes
Peter's admonition to be ready to make a defense for the hope that is in us

serves as a sound starting point for developing topics and themes for apologetic sermons. In an earlier time hope probably would not have been the starting point for most discussions of apologetic themes. As noted earlier, apologists often began with the assumption that they would present Christian faith through logical argumentation. Remember that today's hearers do not favor protracted arguments; to be truthful, most postmoderns would not understand or have their interest held by a logical, linear argument. Today's generations think *mosaically*. Mosaic thinking draws conclusions by seeing a whole in the parts, no matter how or in what order the parts are presented. With a linear argument, you must have an *A* before you can presume a *B*. A culture persuaded through sound bites and short video clips cannot and will not follow the lengthy argumentation that apologists used to employ.

One could certainly make a case for regretting this state of affairs. Nevertheless, all the arguments in the world cannot change the fact that today's listeners do not have the inclination to wade through depths of arguments to be persuaded to Christian faith. They might, however, listen to someone who speaks of *hope* and who shares that hope from life experience.

Once more I want to call attention to Peter's counsel: "Always be ready to make your defense to anyone who demands from you an accounting for the hope that is in you; yet do it with gentleness and reverence." *Gentleness* and *reverence* help set the tone for our apologetic *method*. Accounting for hope helps us set the tone for our apologetic *message*. People respond to hopeful people.

Find ways to communicate specifically the hope you have. Share from personal experience and from the experience of other believers the hope they receive in Christian faith. Being hopeful doesn't mean being naive. Whether in joy or in the pain of tragedy, our faith reverberates with hope. Paul encouraged the Thessalonians by reminding them that the grief they have over the death of their loved ones does not have to be hopeless grief. Even in death there is hope. From the hope of a child born in a manger to the hope of resurrection, not even death quenches our hope.

Hope moves us to the theme of *good news*. Christianity brings good news to the pluralistic conversation table of this present age. World religions, though as ethically demanding as Christian faith, often work out of fatalism and determinism. Some faith systems demand that adherents relinquish all claims to the present world. Others are founded on a pessimistic worldview, challenging their believers to abandon this world because it is inherently evil. Christian faith offers *good news*. It provides an optimistic view of a world laden with sin yet redeemable through Jesus Christ. Christian faith does not require self-flagellation. In Christ we are saved through faith. There is no more hope-filled faith in the world than Christianity; let's use that point to our advantage in talking with others about what we believe.

Good news moves us to the theme of *Jesus Christ*. Jesus Christ should be the subject and object of Christian preaching. He should certainly be the central figure of our apologetic sermons. Our apologetic preaching should be *Christocentric*. The complete and full message of Jesus Christ remains crucial if our apologetic endeavors are to be faithful. I have heard of some seeker-targeted churches—some, not all—that have removed all vestiges of the cross, both physical and verbal, from their gatherings. No mention of Jesus' suffering or death is ever made. They say they don't want to offend seekers with a concept as gruesome and offensive as crucifying someone. While this kind of practice—which could be called deception—may not be widespread among churches, it shows that we will often give in to society's view of success, even when it comes to preaching.

Jesus Christ, and the gospel he preached and lived, remains the heart of our hope. When we give an account of the hope that is ours, the name of Jesus should roll off our lips. If you take nothing else from this book, take this: preach Jesus Christ. But preach him in a way accessible to postmodern ears. Preach him so that people can see him in your words and actions. Share his life and message through illustrations of how he is transforming the world today. You could point to the continued impact of Billy Graham's ministry or the transforming influence of pastor Jim

Cymbala and the Brooklyn Tabernacle on lives of people once broken and empty. The testimonies of people in your church are prime illustrations of the power of Jesus Christ to transform and redeem lives. Preach that! People should know you love Jesus Christ and serve him. They should be able to sense it from your words and actions, from your countenance and your demeanor. The hope we have is grounded in Jesus Christ; our sermons and preaching must model that. Christocentric preaching deals with the entire Christ event, in all of its scandal and gore. Apologetic preaching must be Christocentric.

Along with being Christ-centered in our preaching, we must not shrink from making the claim of the exclusive and inclusive nature of Christ's atoning death. The death of Jesus Christ is God's only offer to humankind for eternal life. Jesus Christ is God's exclusive offer of salvation. Yet the offer is extended to all who will believe. This theological reality will be perhaps the single biggest hurdle or stumblingblock for postmodern non-Christians to overcome. In a culture that wants everyone to be happy, in a cultural milieu where tolerance is upheld as the greatest of virtues, such exclusive claims for Christ sound intolerant. Our apologetic preaching must show why and how Jesus Christ—the incarnate God—becomes the universal atonement for humankind. We must be able to proclaim the exclusive claim of Christ as a universal offer of redemption and forgiveness that other religions and faith systems do not attempt to offer or ultimately claim. Our effectiveness as apologists will stand or fall on our ability to defend this claim.

Jesus Christ offers us opportunity to speak of *God's acting in our world.* The hope we have, the good news we share, is not merely an insurance policy for eternal life. It also has implications for how we live in this complex world. Christianity is not a Sunday-only enterprise. Our Christian faith should go with us into operating and emergency rooms, into board rooms and courtrooms, into classrooms. Our Christian faith should mold who we are. Christian faith is not merely a belief system; it is how we live. Because God continues to work in our world, we have good news. If we didn't believe this, we would be deists who believe that God created the world and set it on its way as a completely autonomous venture. We believe that God remains intimately concerned and involved in the world. John writes, "And the Word became flesh and lived among us" (Jn 1:14). The eternal Creator became human and experienced life as we live it. Then God sent the Holy Spirit to be his continued indwelling and interactive presence in the world. Our culture, fixated on interactive everything, should relate well to this concept.

Other apologetic themes include the purpose of humankind, the reality of evil, the nature of sin, the issue of theodicy, the means of redemption—to name a few. Where there is a question of faith, where there is an issue of doubt, where there is a topic to be explained, where there is an argument to be settled regarding the Christian faith, apologetic preaching has its role.

Developing a Scheduled Plan for Apologetic Preaching

While preaching takes place in a variety of nonchurch settings—hospital chapels, evangelistic meetings, university campuses—the majority of us preach out of some long-term pastoral relationship with our hearers. That means that our preaching goals must cover the gamut of pastoral concerns. For example, while it may be hard to fathom, much of the pastoral care ministry that pastors offer takes place on Sunday mornings. With the busyness of church members and the vast demands on a pastor's time, most of us have limited the amount of time we're able to spend doing one-on-one pastoral care. Along with formal pastoral care opportunities, pastoral care also takes place in various everyday encounters pastors have with parishioners, and rightly so. But a large amount of care can and is offered through the preaching ministry of parish ministers.

Likewise, Sunday mornings offer times to share good news through apologetic preaching to seekers in our midst. As I noted in *Evangelistic Preaching That Connects*, we must intentionally proclaim and offer the gospel message from our pulpits to those whose empty lives cry out for a God-sized answer. Week by week, preachers step to the pulpit to challenge congregations to become engaged in everything from community ministries to discipleship training to fellowship and growth opportunities to world mission endeavors. From local church programs to denominational emphases, our preaching agenda is set and established. Therefore it becomes essential for preachers to develop preaching plans that intentionally meet the theological needs of their specific congregations.

The Christian year lends itself to the development of series of apologetic sermons. Christmas and Easter seasons are times when a religious and Christian sensitivity spreads in the air. People are more likely to come to church on Christmas and Easter than at any other times of the year. It would behoove us, assuming that many who come have questions and doubts about the veracity of our faith, to preach apologetic sermons offering a clear presentation and defense of the gospel. We want those who enter our sanctuary to be clear when they leave about why we are a hopeful people.

Obviously we want to do that with gentleness and reverence. It is probably not a good thing to say to your Easter crowd, "Nice to see many of you again. I haven't seen you since Christmas." That approach would violate Peter's concern for apologetics with gentleness. On the other side, though, we should not apologize or be ashamed of the unique character of the message we as Christians proclaim. While we want to offer a defense for—a reason for—the hope we have, we don't have to be defensive about it. Our success is measured by our faithfulness in telling the story, telling what we know, and leaving the conversion process to the Holy Spirit.

We can and should highlight the uniqueness of the Christ event when preaching during these two key Christian calendar events. The miraculous circumstances of Jesus' birth give opportunity to present and defend the unequaled claim of Christians that Jesus personifies God's only way to saving knowledge of him. John's claim that the eternal Word became human and walked and lived on earth constitutes the message of Christmas. In the pluralistic culture in which we minister, we often tiptoe around our faith's claim to exclusive salvation in Jesus Christ. Our fear that such a claim will offend someone too often keeps us from offering the absolute good news our world desperately needs. Christmas offers the apologist the opportunity to frame the holiday within the orthodox understanding that at Christmas Christians celebrate God's coming into the world in flesh and blood. The very context of the season offers an apologetic opportunity.

The Easter celebration likewise presents the apologetic preacher with a context to make a sound defense of Christian faith. In our media-saturated world no one escapes exposure to Christian images around Eastertide. Newspapers advertise special church programs focusing on Palm Sunday, Good Friday and Easter Sunday. Easter celebrations in the Vatican and Jerusalem become part of the evening news, often making the front page of newspapers around the world. Here lie rich opportunities for apologetic preaching to clearly delineate the unique character of Christian belief, to clarify misconceptions and false notions, and to reframe people's impressions about the veracity of the crucifixion of Jesus and his bodily resurrection. We should feel less fearful of offending someone with the ubiquitous images of Easter so readily visible to people.

Preaching apologetically at Christmas and Easter—including the seasons of Advent and Lent—certainly fits Peter's call to be ready to make a defense for the hope that we have in Christ. Christmas and Easter offer ready-made opportunities to preach apologetic sermons. To neglect them as apologetic possibilities is woefully wrong.

Other important dates on the Christian calendar, not as celebrated, still give opportunities to share gospel truth and to make a case for Christian faith. Certainly the Thanksgiving holiday can lend itself to apologetic emphasis. Christian hope builds on our grateful relationship with our loving Father. What better way to express that than through the national celebration of Thanksgiving? Other Christian calendar days that could be used apologetically include Pentecost, All Saints' Day, All Souls' Day and Reformation Sunday. While these holidays are not all celebrated by the public at large, they will, to the attuned preacher, offer opportunities to frame sermons that will help get the case out for Jesus Christ.

Another approach to developing a scheduled plan for apologetic preaching is to analyze your preaching plan over the past twelve to eighteen months. Evaluate the types of series or sermons you've preached. Ask yourself some questions like these:

☐ If unchurched people had heard those sermons, would they be better informed about the truth claims of Christians?

☐ Would seekers know what Christians believe?

☐ Would unchurched people understand *why* Christians believe what they believe?

☐ Would detractors of the faith have had their objections addressed?

☐ Did my preaching offer an accounting for the hope that is in me?

By analyzing where you've been sermonically, you'll be better able to prayerfully project a future preaching plan that will include apologetic sermons.

Given the cultural milieu in which we find ourselves, sermons must presume an apologetic tone. People, even churched people, are often ignorant about what they believe and why they believe it. Every so often my attention will be caught by a statistic showing how little churchgoing people know about their faith. I think to myself, *Say it ain't so!* In a recent seminar I attended, George Barna cited appalling statistics reflecting the ignorance among the ranks of evangelical Christians about what they believe. He suggested we survey our congregations with basic faith questions. He predicted we'd be appalled by the results. I never did the survey. I took his word for it.

I have begun an aggressive apologetic preaching approach with my congregation. I ask myself as I prepare the sermon, *Will the congregation be better able to offer a defense of their faith as a result of hearing this sermon? Am I strengthening their faith and helping them prevent their Christianity from being warped?* After taking this approach for a time I plan to invite Barna to survey the congregation and see how we're doing.

Apologetic preaching must be a natural part of the mix of sermonic theology you share with your congregation to help them grow and remain rooted in their faith.

Apologetic Preaching and Evangelism

In discussions with thoroughgoing apologists and in talks with accomplished evangelists, you might get the impression that the roads of these two disciplines never meet. In fact, you might even get the notion that they should not converge. But this is like the argument over which is correct, Paul's admonition to justification by faith or James's concern that faith without works is dead. In the latter discussion it has become clear that Paul and James' arguments complement each other. In Christ we are justified by faith, and the reality of that faith becomes demonstrated by good works reflected in our lives. Likewise, to argue that apologetics and evangelism remain somehow at odds with each other misses the complementary relationship between these two critical disciplines. In terms of what is needed for the third millennium, I would like to make a case for a contingent relationship between apologetic preaching and evangelism.

My book *Evangelistic Preaching That Connects* used Richard S. Armstrong's definition for *evangelism:* "Evangelism is proclaiming in word and deed the good news of the kingdom of God and calling people to repentance, to personal faith in Jesus Christ as Lord and Savior, to active membership in the church, and to obedient service in the world."[1] And in the current cultural climate of pluralism and relativism—what one might call a neopagan culture—the ground for evangelism will have to be properly furrowed and prepared by effective apologetics.

Postmodern intellectuals appear too "politically correct" to take up issues of sin and repentance as a starting point in the discussion. Yet for Christians, the conversation will never be much of a conversation if it never gets around to humanity's sin and the need for redemption. A case for Christian faith will first have to be made. In other words, evangelists will have to be ready to make a defense to those who demand from them an accounting for the hope that they have. Such will be the role of apologetics. Some have called this strategy one of preevangelism. I prefer to refer to it as an actual part of the evangelistic endeavor of the church. For the third millennium, apologetics and evangelism must go hand in hand. Neglect either and the Christian conversation with the postmodern world falters.

How then can apologetic preaching begin the evangelism task? Again, as I wrote in *Evangelistic Preaching That Connects*, evangelism—the sharing of the good news offered by Jesus Christ—is sharing with people the hope that we Christians carry within us. That hope, according to Paul, "is Christ in you, the hope of glory" (Col 1:27). Apologetic preaching, as characterized throughout this book, offers a thoughtful and intentional presentation of Christian faith as a viable alternative to the myriad religious options available within postmodern culture. My contention is that those options will grow as the new millennium advances. For Christians to assume they can do business as usual and remain a player in the world of multiple religious options borders on the ridiculous.

Apologetic preaching unapologetically describes and proclaims the essentials of Christian faith. It makes a case for such foundational Christian doctrines as God's personal intervention in world history, the humanity and divinity of Christ, the salvific effect of the cross, Christ's bodily resurrection, and the Holy Spirit's presence in the life of believers. Offering a word of good news—evangelism—apologetic preaching describes the human condition and God's providential provision for it. Apologetic preaching makes the case for the gospel. It describes why the world needs salvation; it explains why individuals need salvation. In a world marked by skepticism of organized religion, apologetic preaching breaks the ice and makes the need for good news tenable.

As good news, apologetic preaching tells those who've never heard and reminds those who've forgotten or have taken it for granted that God, the Creator and sustainer, desires a relationship with us because of who he is. God is a God of love; love requires relationship. Relationships sing from a stance of hope. Remember, apologetics builds its case around the hope that exudes from a Christian's life. People want to know what makes us tick. Why are we hopeful? They want to know why we can face grief without pathologic despair. People don't understand why we have an optimistic outlook when others view our world through the lenses of pessimism. They want to know how we cope with real reality. Apologetic preaching presents the case for our hopeful relationship with God, no matter our walk in life. Authentic evangelistic and apologetic preaching brings good news to the poor, proclaims release to captives, restores sight to those who are blind, lets the oppressed go free, and proclaims the year of the Lord's favor.

The Bible is the good news book. It opens with a picture of God taking the initiative, hovering over a formless void where darkness and chaos reign, and God speaks creation into existence. The chaos is harnessed and transformed by God's creative Word. We hear of each new day breaking forth as God delights in what's taking place: "And God saw that it was good." The anticipation builds from sky to land and seas, to plants and trees, to the sun and moon, to fish and fowl and wild animals and livestock. As if following the modern adage about saving the best for last, the narrator proclaims some good news: "Then God said, 'Let us make humankind in our image, according to our likeness.' . . . So God created humankind in his image, in the image of God he created them; male and female he created them" (Gen 1:26-27). Then God blessed them.

The creation—with its fauna, fish, fowl and people—pleased God. The first chapter of the Bible is rich with good news. It tells of God's intentional creative acts, of the human partnership with God in sustaining the creation, and the essence of good news that we are created in the very image and likeness of God. At a time when people struggle with the need to make sense out of life, when they long for meaning and acceptance, when many seem lonely and isolated, what better news than to discover we're created in God's image? Christian apologetics shouts from the mountaintop that people don't have to strive to be somebody, they don't have to die of exhaustion making a name for themselves.

One could say that evangelism proclaims the *what* of the gospel and apologetics explains the *why*. While this comparison may be an oversimplification, I think it makes the point. When we are speaking of Christ's redemptive action, it becomes nearly impossible to separate the *what* from the *why*. *What* God did through Jesus Christ is woven thoroughly into *why* he acted as he did. Hence the integral relationship between evangelism and apologetics. Apologetic preaching takes on the appearance of evangelism when it helps people see that the reason—*why*—God gave his only Son—*what*—was that he loved the world. And that's good news indeed.

Apologetic Preaching to the Church

Typically, Christian apologetics presumes a hostile or at least an unsympathetic audience. Yet in the current postmodern, post-Christian era there remains a role for an apologetic voice even within the context of Christian worship. Many contemporary believers are uncertain of the basis for their faith and have no ability to give a defense of their faith to others. Many church people need to have their faith strengthened and grounded. To many within the walls of the typical church, there appears to be a blind allegiance to a church, its programs or its denominational moorings. Tragically, I fear a survey of contemporary Christianity would reveal a church membership with little reflection on or understanding of the implications of Christian faith. If the typical congregant were asked to make a defense for the hope they hold, I'm afraid the results would be less than admirable.

Perhaps the reason for this malady is that Christianity in our context has led a peaceful existence, not exposed to the harassment and persecution that many Christians around the world experience. There seems little need to defend one's faith when there is never any offense to it. Perhaps the reason is mere apathy. American Christians, as a whole, seem less zealous about their faith than their counterparts in other places around the world. Because of an inherent self-reliance Americans possess, even reliance on God feels, perhaps subconsciously, like a weakness. No doubt other believers around the world are better able to defend their faith because they have *had* to defend it.

As I mentioned earlier, I had the privilege to teach a course in preaching at the Evangelical Christian-Baptist Seminary in Moscow, Russia. On one particular Sunday several colleagues and I worshiped at the Central Baptist Church in Moscow. Russian Baptist worship services typically last two to two and a half hours. They include a lot of singing, several sermons and a lot of praying. During the service, which was being interpreted to us, the pastor called on the congregation to pray. At this point the older women of the church—known as the *babushkas*—left their pews and gathered at the front of the sanctuary and down the aisle, circling large pillars that lined the huge interior. Joining hands, they gently rocked and prayed inaudible prayers.

A colleague leaned over to me and whispered, "For the past seventy years these are the women who prayed communism out of Russia." I think he was right. They literally had to defend their faith—sometimes overtly, other times covertly—on a daily basis. They lived and died by their faith in Jesus Christ. Their faith was not a Sunday-only proposition; they walked daily facing life and death crises. In those circumstances, Christian faith grows because it is regularly exercised.

The level of comfort experienced by American Christians is probably the culprit for our apologetic feebleness. Whatever the case, apologetic preaching to the church is a needed theological and pastoral discipline. Christianity will not survive into the third millennium with believers who cannot articulate and make a defense of their faith. Aloof, apathetic, comfortable Christianity will not survive in the twenty-first century. If pastoral preaching's goal is to *comfort the afflicted*, then certainly the goal of apologetic preaching becomes to *afflict the comfortable*.

If apologetics is based on the premise that Christians should be able to make a defense to anyone who demands from them an accounting for the hope they have, then a key role of apologetic preaching is to provide believers with the wherewithal to make that defense. In other words, apologetic preaching becomes basic training for church members to present and defend their Christian faith. It could be argued that the pulpit is not the proper venue for such instruction. After all, the pulpit is the place for mass appeals. I would agree that small group training would provide a better opportunity to discuss, perhaps even role-play, the various strategies necessary for building a community of faith that can both present and defend its beliefs. However, the gathering of folk in worship remains the best venue to allow a congregation as a whole to know and be exposed to the issues facing them as believers—even as corporate believers. Statements made from the pulpit carry extra weight; this should not be taken lightly. If you're not sure it is true, why is it that every organization and group in the church wants their announcement made from the pulpit, even those announcements that are printed in the weekly worship bulletin? People can read all about it in the bulletin, but when they hear the senior pastor or another staff person plead the cause, it carries the imprimatur of the church's leadership. That endorsement carries clout.

The pulpit can be used to inaugurate a major churchwide apologetic emphasis. At Immanuel Baptist Church, before we began teaching *Becoming a Contagious Christian* through small groups, I taught an overview of the eight sessions during our Sunday-evening worship services. We used the video that comes with the material; we also had our drama team act out several vignettes. We had excellent participation because our usual Sunday-night congregation was present—about 350 people. We had a captive audience, so to speak. Had we merely offered the seminar in small group format, many would have avoided the course because its content deals with sharing one's faith, a topic that makes many people uncomfortable. Once we had offered the inaugural series as a churchwide event, the later small group offerings were well attended, and our people are now becoming "contagious Christians." By using the pulpit to highlight the importance of the subject matter, we were able to effect a better churchwide outcome. (By the way, *Becoming a Contagious Christian*[2] is an excellent apologetic and evangelistic resource.)

Apologetic preaching to the church should cover a wide range of topics and issues. You should spend time surveying the many faith options available to people today and showing how Christianity is the only viable option before God. Many contemporary believers have been taken in by the popular axiom that it doesn't matter what you believe as long as you believe something. Apologetic preaching to the church must debunk that notion.

Your apologetic preaching within the church context should deal with both content issues and process issues. In other words, *what* is it we are defending and *how* do we go about defending it? Begin with the basics; do not assume that your congregation understands Christian faith. Always begin with the assumption that they have amnesia and have forgotten what they knew. This way new believers and older believers will learn and grow together.

Be careful not to be condescending in using this approach. Fred Craddock says that in many cases authentic learning is *recognizing* something we already know experientially. Your apologetic preaching should teach and encourage your congregation to engage people in conversations about their religious beliefs. We cannot offer a defense for the hope we have if no one ever asks or if we don't display hope!

Apologetic preaching that encourages the church to participate in Christian apologetics will be a vital force to move the church forward in the third millennium. Effective churches will take this part of the apologetic task seriously.

Planning Worship Services with Apologetic Emphases

A general word about worship will be helpful to frame our discussion. The term *worship* comes from the Anglo-Saxon *weorthscipe*, meaning to assign ultimate value. Worship, then, is the ascribing ultimate worth to God. All that we do and say when a congregation gathers should be done and said in remembrance that we have gathered to offer our best selves to God. I am not sure of the source, but one definition of *faith* goes like this: "Faith is giving all that I know and understand about myself to all that I know and understand about God." Shifting the saying slightly, could we say *worship* is giving all that we know and understand about ourselves to all that we know and understand about God?

God is the focus of our worship. One helpful model of worship, often attributed to the Danish philosopher Søren Kierkegaard, sees the congregation as the actor, the worship leaders as prompters and God as the audience.[3] This model suggests that we prepare corporate worship focused on God as the One who will receive our worship. All that we say and do comes together as a living offering to God (see Rom 12:1-2). In other words, the purpose of worship is not to please or entertain a congregation. When a congregation's wishes and whims dictate the hows and whys of worship, it is time to reevaluate our worship practice. I believe the congregation is a vital part of worship, but as *participants in*, not *recipients of*, worship.

There are vertical and horizontal dimensions of worship. The vertical dimension establishes our upward relationship with God. The horizontal dimension demonstrates the relationship we have with others made possible by our relationship with God. If the horizontal dimension of our worship is faulty, our vertical dimension will be thwarted. That's why Jesus said, "So when you are offering your gift at the altar, if you remember that your brother or sister has something against you, leave your gift there before the altar and go; first be reconciled to your brother or sister, and then come and offer your gift" (Mt 5:23-24). Our horizontal relationship with others reflects our vertical relationship with God.

With that said, what are some practical ways participation is accomplished? The gift of music is an integral part of corporate worship, enabling and enhancing all of the elements of the service. Music is produced by congregational singing, choirs, soloists, ensembles of various sizes, and instrumentalists. Music in worship should be uplifting and inspiring. It must also be filled with cognitive images that expand our understanding of who God is and the work God has for us in the kingdom. Music for a service that has an apologetic emphasis—whether congregational songs or music sung by a choir or praise team—should be chosen so that the words help to carry the overall worship theme.

The praise of God is an important element in corporate worship. In a service with an apologetic flair, praise and worship music becomes essential. Unchurched people don't understand and often have a negative predisposition to the traditional music they might hear in church. It is foreign to their ears. Traditional church music often lacks the cultural relevance that postmodern seekers understand as authentic. Again, choose praise and worship music and choruses that will help carry the theme of the entire service.

Public prayers are an important part of corporate worship. Again, to maintain an apologetic emphasis in the current cultural milieu means that even the choice of our prayer words becomes important. I'm not sure why it is, but when some people begin to pray in public, they immediately fall back to King James English. They think that addressing God as *thee* and *thou* somehow adds an air of reverence. That's an interesting assumption, because in 1611 *thee* and *thou* were colloquial pronouns. Though our prayers are addressed to God, we must remember that in a public context we have a responsibility to help others pray. If the words we choose become a stumbling block, we've defeated our apologetic purposes.

One of the important aspects of worship is the public reading of Scripture. To maintain an apologetic tone, develop a variety of ways the Bible can be read. For example, a narrative passage of Scripture can be read by the praise team, with different members reading the narrator and characters' parts. A responsive reading can be creatively written and printed in the bulletin or projected. The congregation then takes part in the reading of the Word. Vary the translations used, to help hearers see that the Word comes to us in the dynamic of the language we currently speak. Eugene Petersen's *The Message* is a wonderful contemporary translation to use. Those who worship with us, even when the service has a decidedly apologetic tone, should know beyond a shadow of a doubt that our authority to preach and worship comes from beyond us. We should not be ashamed to hold high the Bible, for it points to Christ, the Son of the living God.

When a worship service ends, a key question should be, Have we, corporately and individually, encountered God? The church in worship finds itself uplifted, empowered, motivated to love one another, and prompted to love the world because it has met and honored God. When a congregation meets God humbly in prayer, adoration and submission, it is changed. Having met God, we can no longer pass over injustice with a fleeting glance Having met God, we begin to live now under a kingdom ethic. Having met

God, we shift our church agenda from inside to outside.

Like a cool drink after a long walk, worship quenches the thirst of the church that truly worships God. Jesus said, echoing the Torah, "You shall love the Lord your God with all your heart, and with all your soul, and with all your mind" (Mt 22:37). No other admonition can so transform the church, nurture its ministries, revitalize its fellowship as the encounter God makes available to us through worship.

As a result of worship the church finds itself empowered to move beyond its walls, finding its neighbors and loving them. That, after all, was Jesus' second word: "You shall love your neighbor as yourself" (Mt 22:39). Yes the worship of God prepares the church to meet the world, and to give our defense to anyone who demands from us an accounting for the hope that we have.

Epilogue

We began by asking: Is it possible to preach mystery in an age of information? Can we preach hope in an era of skepticism? Is it possible to preach confidence in a time of doubt? Can we share our message of truth in a climate of relativism? Step by step this book has attempted to answer these questions and provide practicing preachers, students of preaching and seminarians a tool to use as they face the daunting task of presenting Christ to a postmodern world. The ultimate question becomes, Can we preach Christ to a postmodern world? My answer, of course, is yes—unapologetically, *yes*!

Notes

Chapter 1: Apologizing for God

[1]Thomas Oden, "The Death of Modernity and Postmodern Evangelical Spirituality," in *The Challenge of Postmodernism: An Evangelical Engagement*, ed. David S. Dockery (Wheaton, Ill.: Victor/BridgePoint, 1995), p. 20.

[2]David G. Buttrick, "Speaking Between Times: Homiletics in a Postmodern World," paper presented at the annual meeting of the Academy of Homiletics, Durham, North Carolina, December 1–3, 1994, p. 2.

[3]Diogenes Allen, quoted in Alister McGrath, *Intellectuals Don't Need God and Other Modern Myths* (Grand Rapids, Mich.: Zondervan, 1993), p. 177.

[4]Buttrick, "Speaking Between Times," p. 3.

[5]Oden, "Death of Modernity," p. 24.

[6]Ibid., p. 29.

[7]Carl F. H. Henry, "Postmodernism: The New Spectre," in *The Challenge of Postmodernism: An Evangelical Engagement*, ed. David S. Dockery (Wheaton, Ill.: Victor/BridgePoint, 1995), p. 41.

[8]Robert Bellah et al., *Habits of the Heart: Individualism and Commitment in American Life* (Berkeley: University of California Press, 1985).

[9]David S. Dockery, "The Challenge of Postmodernism," in *The Challenge of Postmodernism: An Evangelical Engagement*, ed. David S. Dockery (Wheaton, Ill.: Victor/BridgePoint, 1995), p. 15.

[10]Stanley Grenz, "Star Trek and the Next Generation: Postmodernism and the Future of Evangelical Theology," in *The Challenge of Postmodernism: An Evangelical Engagement*, ed. David S. Dockery (Wheaton, Ill.: Victor/BridgePoint, 1995), p. 99.

[11]McGrath, *Intellectuals Don't Need God*, p. 81.

[12]David Buttrick, classroom lecture, Vanderbilt Divinity School, spring 1995.

[13]Bernard Ramm, *Varieties of Christian Apologetics* (Grand Rapids, Mich.: Baker, 1961), p. 13.

[14]McGrath, *Intellectuals Don't Need God*, p. 68.

[15]Ibid., p. 341.

[16]Thomas C. Oden, *After Modernity . . . What? Agenda for Theology* (Grand Rapids, Mich.: Zondervan, 1989), pp. 168-69.

[17]Grenz, "Star Trek," p. 99.

[18]Karl Barth, *Evangelical Theology: An Introduction*, trans. Grover Foley (New York: Holt, Rinehart & Winston, 1963).

[19]Peter Kreeft and Ronald K. Tacelli, *Handbook of Christian Apologetics* (Downers Grove, Ill.: InterVarsity Press, 1994). While much in their book is very helpful, some of their presuppositions concerning the role of reasoning in apologetics reflect stereotypical modern/Western modes of thought.

[20]McGrath, *Intellectuals Don't Need God*, p. 56.

Chapter 2: Proclaiming Mystery in an Age of Information

[1]Tony Campolo, quoted in "Campolo: Prepare Churches for the Post-modern World," *Western Recorder* 170, no. 46 (November 1996): 1.

[2]Karl Barth, *Evangelical Theology: An Introduction*, trans. Grover Foley (New York: Holt, Rinehart & Winston, 1963).

[3]C. S. Lewis, *Mere Christianity* (New York: Macmillan, 1943), pp. 58–59.

[4]Edward G. Dobson, "Taking Politics out of the Sanctuary: The Church's Energy Should Be Spent Redeeming the Lost, Not Rallying Against Them," *Christianity Today*, May 20, 1996.

[5]"Resurrection Key in Christian Faiths," *Lexington Herald-Leader*, April 6, 1997, p. A11.

[6]Laura Schlessinger, "Religious Services Can Elevate and Energize," *Lexington Herald-Leader*, March 25, 1997, p. 5.

Chapter 3: Proclaiming Hope in an Era of Skepticism

[1]Stanley Hauerwas and William H. Willimon, *Resident Aliens: A Provocative Christian Assessment of Culture and Ministry for People Who Know That Something Is Wrong* (Nashville: Abingdon, 1989), pp. 15–17.

[2]William H. Willimon, *Acts,* Interpretation (Atlanta: John Knox Press, 1988), p. 29.

[3]Ibid., p. 33.

[4]Ibid.

[5]Frederick Buechner, "A Sprig of Hope," in *A Chorus of Witnesses: Model Sermons for Today's Preacher*, ed. Thomas G. Long and Cornelius Plantinga Jr. (Grand Rapids, Mich.: Eerdmans, 1994), p. 231.

[6]John Claypool, *Tracks of a Fellow Struggler* (Waco, Tex.: Word, 1974), p. 55.

[7]Frank Tupper, *A Scandalous Providence: The Jesus Story of the Compassion of God* (Macon, Ga.: Mercer University Press, 1995), pp. 79-81.

Chapter 4: Proclaiming Confidence in a Time of Doubt
[1]C. E. B. Cranfield, *The Apostles' Creed: A Faith to Live By* (Grand Rapids, Mich.: Eerdmans, 1993), p. 5.

[2]The modern version of the Apostles' Creed as rendered in ibid., p. 3.

[3]*The Baptist Faith and Message* (Nashville: Lifeway Christian Resources, 1998), p. 8.

[4]Ibid., p. 10.

[5]Bob Briner, *Deadly Detours: Seven Noble Causes That Keep Christians from Changing the World* (Grand Rapids, Mich.: Zondervan, 1996), p. 10.

Chapter 5: Proclaiming Truth in a Climate of Relativism
[1]John Killinger, "What Is Truth? Or Shirley MacLaine, Meet the Master," in *Best Sermons One*, ed. James W. Cox (San Francisco: Harper & Row, 1988), pp. 133–39.

Chapter 6: Proclaiming Jesus Christ to a Postmodern World
[1]John Shelby Spong, *Why Christianity Must Change or Die: A Bishop Speaks to Believers in Exile* (San Francisco: Harper, 1999).

[2]Tex Sample, *U.S. Lifestyles and Mainline Churches: A Key to Reaching People in the 90s* (Louisville, Ky.: Westminster John Knox, 1990), pp. 42–43.

[3]Kenneth A. Myers, *All God's Children and Blue Suede Shoes: Christians and Popular Culture* (Wheaton, Ill.: Crossway, 1989).

[4]J. B. Phillips, *Your God Is Too Small* (New York: Macmillan, 1961).

[5]Hans-Georg Gadamer, *Truth and Method* (New York: Crossroad, 1988).

[6]John Killinger, *Preaching to a Church in Crisis: A Homiletic for the Last Days of the Mainline Church* (Lima, Ohio: CSS Publishing, 1995), pp. 92–93.

Chapter 7: How to Apologize Without Saying You're Sorry
[1]Richard Stoll Armstrong, *The Pastor-Evangelist in the Parish* (Louisville, Ky.: Westminster John Knox, 1990), p. 13.

[2]Bill Hybels and Mark Mittleberg, *Becoming a Contagious Christian,* Willow Creek Resources (Grand Rapids, Mich.: Zondervan, 1994).

[3]For a modification of Kierkegaard's model, see Raymond Bailey, "From Theory to Practice in Worship," *Review & Expositor* 58 (Winter 1983): 34.

Index